Carolyn's mother asked me through Carolyn if I would like a *sushi*. A plate of black and white things were held in front of me. I took one, wide-eyed, and turned it over like a foreign coin. I was biting into one when I saw a kitten crawl up the window screen over the sink. I chewed and the kitten opened its mouth of terror as she crawled higher, wanting in to paw the leftovers from our plates. I looked at Carolyn, who said that the cat was just showing off. I looked up in time to see it fall. It crawled up, then fell again.

We talked for an hour and had apple pie and coffee, slowly. Finally, we got up with Carolyn taking my hand. Slightly embarrassed, I tried to pull away but her grip held me. I let her have her way as she led me down the hallway with her mother right behind me. When I opened the door, I was startled by a kitten clinging to the screen door, its mouth screaming "cat food, dog biscuits, *sushi*. . . ." I opened the door and the kitten, still holding on, whined in the language of hungry animals.

ALSO AVAILABLE IN LAUREL-LEAF BOOKS:

Small Faces

Gary Soto

For Carolyn

Published by
Dell Publishing
a division of
Bantam Doubleday Dell Publishing Group, Inc.
1540 Broadway
New York, New York 10036

Grateful acknowledgement is made to the following publications, in
which some of these essays first appeared: *Imagine, Open Places,
Revista Chicano-Requena,* and *Telescope.*

The author would like to thank Lorraine Aochi, Julian Olivares, and
his wife, Carolyn, for first reading the essays.

These essays were written during the month of December 1983 and
between the months of June and August 1984.

ISBN: 0-440-21553-6

RL:5.3

Reprinted by arrangement with BookStop Literary Agency, on behalf
of the author

Printed in the United States of America

August 1993

10 9 8 7 6 5 4 3 2 1

OPM

Contents

vi   Contents

Like Mexicans

MY GRANDMOTHER gave me bad advice and good advice when I was in my early teens. For the bad advice, she said that I should become a barber because they made good money and listened to the radio all day. "Honey, they don't work como burros," she would say every time I visited her. She made the sound of donkeys braying. "Like that, honey!" For the good advice, she said that I should marry a Mexican girl. "No Okies, hijo"—she would say—"Look my son. He marry one and they fight every day about I don't know what and I don't know what." For her, everyone who wasn't Mexican, black, or Asian were Okies. The French were Okies, the Italians in suits were Okies. When I asked about Jews, whom I had read about, she asked for a picture. I rode home on my bicycle and returned with a calendar depicting the important races of the world. "Pues sí, son Okies también!" she said, nodding her head. She waved the calendar away and we went to the living room where she lectured me on the virtues of the Mexican girl: first, she could cook and, second, she acted like a woman, not a man, in her husband's home. She said she would tell me about a third when I got a little older.

I asked my mother about it—becoming a barber and marrying Mexican. She was in the kitchen. Steam curled from a pot of boiling beans, the radio was on, looking as squat as a loaf of bread. "Well, if you want to be a barber—they say they make good money." She slapped a round steak with a knife, her glasses slipping down with each strike. She stopped and looked up. "If you find a good Mexican girl, marry her of course." She returned to slapping the meat and I went to the backyard where my brother and David King were sitting on the lawn feeling the inside of their cheeks.

"This is what girls feel like," my brother said, rubbing the inside of his cheek. David put three fingers inside his mouth and scratched. I ignored them and climbed the back fence to see my best friend, Scott, a second-generation Okie. I called him, and his mother pointed to the side of the house where his bedroom was a small aluminum trailer, the kind you gawk at when they're flipped over on the freeway, wheels spinning in the air. I went around to find Scott pitching horseshoes.

I picked up a set of rusty ones and joined him. While we played, we talked about school and friends and record albums. The horseshoes scuffed up dirt, sometimes ringing the iron that threw out a meager shadow like a sundial. After three argued-over games, we pulled two oranges apiece from his tree and started down the alley still talking school and friends and record albums. We pulled more oranges from the alley and talked about who we would marry. "No offense, Scott," I said with an orange slice in my mouth, "but I would never marry an Okie." We walked in step, almost touching, with a sled of shadows dragging behind us. "No offense, Gary," Scott said, "but I would *never* marry a Mexican." I looked at him: a fang of orange slice showed from his munching mouth. I didn't think anything of it. He had his girl and I had mine. But our seventh-grade vision was the same: to marry, get jobs, buy cars and maybe a house if we had money left over.

We talked about our future lives until, to our surprise, we were on the downtown mall, two miles from home. We bought a bag of popcorn at Penney's and sat on a bench near the fountain watching Mexican and Okie girls pass. "That one's mine." I pointed with my chin when a girl with eyebrows arched into black rainbows ambled by. "She's cute," Scott said about a girl with yellow hair and a mouthful of gum. We dreamed aloud, our chins busy pointing out girls. We agreed that we couldn't wait to become men and lift them onto our laps.

But the woman I married was not Mexican but Japanese. It was a surprise to me. For years, I went about wide-eyed in my search for the brown girl in a white dress at a dance. I searched the playground at the baseball diamond. When the girls raced for grounders, their hair bounced like something that couldn't be caught. When they sat together in the lunchroom, heads pressed together, I knew they were talking about us Mexican guys. I saw them and dreamed them. I threw my face into my pillow, making up sentences that were good as in the movies.

But when I was twenty, I fell in love with this other girl who worried my mother, who had my grandmother asking once again to see the calendar of the Important Races of the World. I told her I had thrown it away years before. I took a much-glanced-at snapshot from my wallet. We looked at it together, in silence. Then grandma reclined in her chair, lit a cigarette, and said, "Es pretty." She blew and asked with all her worry pushed up to her forehead: "Chinese?"

I was in love and there was no looking back. She was the one. I told my mother who was slapping hamburger into patties. "Well, sure if you want to marry her," she said. But the more I talked, the more concerned she became. Later I began to worry. Was it all a mistake? "Marry a Mexican girl," I heard my mother say in my mind. I heard it at breakfast. I heard it over math problems, between Western Civilization and cultural geography. But then one afternoon while I was hitchhiking home from school, it struck me like a baseball in the back: my mother wanted me to marry someone of my own social class —a poor girl. I considered my fiancee, Carolyn, and she didn't look poor, though I knew she came from a family of farm workers and pull-yourself-up-by-your-bootstraps ranchers. I asked my brother, who was marrying Mexican poor that fall, if I should marry a poor girl. He screamed "Yeah" above his terrible guitar playing in his bedroom. I considered

my sister who had married Mexican. Cousins were
dating Mexican. Uncles were remarrying poor
women. I asked Scott, who was still my best friend,
and he said, "She's too good for you, so you better
not."

I worried about it until Carolyn took me home to
meet her parents. We drove in her Plymouth until the
houses gave way to farms and ranches and finally her
house fifty feet from the highway. When we pulled
into the drive, I panicked and begged Carolyn to
make a U-turn and go back so we could talk about it
over a soda. She pinched my cheek, calling me a
"silly boy." I felt better, though, when I got out of
the car and saw the house: the chipped paint, a
cracked window, boards for a walk to the back door.
There were rusting cars near the barn. A tractor with
a net of spiderwebs under a mulberry. A field. A bale
of barbed wire like children's scribbling leaning
against an empty chicken coop. Carolyn took my
hand and pulled me to my future mother-in-law who
was coming out to greet us.

We had lunch: sandwiches, potato chips, and iced
tea. Carolyn and her mother talked mostly about
neighbors and the congregation at the Japanese
Methodist Church in West Fresno. Her father, who
was in khaki work clothes, excused himself with a
wave that was almost a salute and went outside. I
heard a truck start, a dog bark, and then the truck
rattle away.

Carolyn's mother offered another sandwich, but I
declined with a shake of my head and a smile. I

looked around when I could, when I was not saying
over and over that I was a college student, hinting
that I could take care of her daughter. I shifted my
chair. I saw newspapers piled in corners, dusty cereal
boxes and vinegar bottles in corners. The wallpaper
was bubbled from rain that had come in from a bad
roof. Dust. Dust lay on lamp shades and window
sills. These people are just like Mexicans, I thought.
Poor people.

Carolyn's mother asked me through Carolyn if I
would like a *sushi*. A plate of black and white things
were held in front of me. I took one, wide-eyed, and
turned it over like a foreign coin. I was biting into
one when I saw a kitten crawl up the window screen
over the sink. I chewed and the kitten opened its
mouth of terror as she crawled higher, wanting in to
paw the leftovers from our plates. I looked at Carolyn, who said that the cat was just showing off. I
looked up in time to see it fall. It crawled up, then fell
again.

We talked for an hour and had apple pie and coffee, slowly. Finally, we got up with Carolyn taking
my hand. Slightly embarrassed, I tried to pull away
but her grip held me. I let her have her way as she led
me down the hallway with her mother right behind
me. When I opened the door, I was startled by a
kitten clinging to the screen door, its mouth screaming "cat food, dog biscuits, *sushi*. . . ." I opened the
door and the kitten, still holding on, whined in the
language of hungry animals. When I got into Carolyn's car, I looked back: the cat was still clinging. I

asked Carolyn if it was possibly hungry, but she said the cat was being silly. She started the car, waved to her mother, and bounced us over the rain-poked drive, patting my thigh for being her lover baby. Carolyn waved again. I looked back, waving, then gawking at a window screen where there were now three kittens clawing and screaming to get in. Like Mexicans, I thought. I remembered the Molinas and how the cats clung to their screens—cats they shot down with squirt guns. On the highway, I felt happy, pleased by it all. I patted Carolyn's thigh. Her people were like Mexicans, only different.

IT'S DIFFICULT telling secrets, especially if you're married as I've been for nine years. Last night while my wife stepped from the bathroom, pink from a shower, I sat in bed thumbing through a magazine and thinking about what I've not told my wife, from would-be lovers to my small fears, like waking up to find spiders staring at me from inside my shoes.

My wife stood before the mirror, her skin slowly cooling under a nightgown, and worked a face cream into the little lines around her eyes that will someday mesh into other lines. I watched this nightly ritual: she dabbed into a jar, made circular motions with two fingers from her brow to her throat, and dabbed again. She plucked at her eyebrows and studied her face as if she were meeting someone new. Finally she came to bed. We read together: a novel for her and a magazine for me. I adjusted my pillow, fixed another on top, and cocked my elbow so that my head rested in my palm. But after a while my neck hurt, so I lay on my stomach with my magazine in front of me.

But I couldn't concentrate on the words or even skim the cartoons and the ads that announced shiny things I needed. I rolled onto my back, eyes on the ceiling. My mouth slowly curled into a smile when I thought of a secret I could tell my wife, a secret that would not hurt but only amaze. I wanted to make her put down her book, screw up her face, and think, "Who did I marry?"

I wanted to roll onto my stomach and, with a squeezing hand on her hip, snuggle my face into her neck and say, "Honey, let me tell you a story." I rolled onto my side but didn't say anything. I smiled. She turned her face to me, smiling. An hour later we were asleep.

I have a friend whose father enjoyed a secret for twenty years. He is a big rancher who talks loudly, who slaps his thighs at Henny Youngman jokes, drinks two beers at once, and talks about the money he keeps in his cellar (gold bars next to homemade jams) to anyone who will listen. But he is also a man who can keep quiet, saying few words when everyone else is talking up a storm. He let go of his secret one slow Saturday when he said to his family, "Let's go for a drive." His wife ignored him and kept piling rinsed dishes into a rack. His children went outside to climb into trees. But the father packed a bag of fruit—oranges and apples—and took down blankets from the hall closet. In a few minutes his family was shooed into the car, their faces pressed to the windows as they sped down a road that was new to them. An hour later they were at a small rural airstrip. He pointed to a yellow plane. The children raced to be first, ducking their heads as they climbed into the back. The children jumped up and down. The wife was scared, then mad, as she demanded that he stop acting like a fool. He slapped his thighs, started the engine, and gunned the plane down the runway until it lifted with a bounce that had everyone screaming to get out. The sky went blue; the trees seemed no bigger than puddles. The plane climbed toward their town of Exeter, and buzzed their house to the wife's embarrassment because the neighbors had come out to gawk.

His secret was that he could fly a plane. The secret I wanted to share with my wife was that I had once rented an apartment in San Francisco. Better yet, I shared an apartment with a woman who had recently come back from a four-year stay in Greece. It was a harmless arrangement. She had a bedroom and I had my own, though often we shared lunches: soups and avocado-and-tomato sandwiches at a small kitchen table where we talked softly as lovers. But we weren't. I was married and she was engaged to a Bulgarian living in Greece. We bit into sandwiches, slurped soup, and talked about the secrets we kept from our better halves.

With a thermos of coffee, we sometimes sat in rickety chairs on the roof, five flights above the noise of traffic. The days were bright. The Golden Gate stood like a harp in the distance and the bay seemed bluer than we could remember. Sailboats moved slowly, or not at all. Smoke rose from freighters. Glare smeared the windows of the apartment buildings on Nob Hill.

Now and then a couple from another roof would look at us and we would look back until they turned away, pointing to something of interest in the not-so-far distance.

I stayed there for a month to find out what it would be like to spend my days in San Francisco. My wife didn't suspect where I went. It was summer, school was out, and my wife thought I spent my mornings reading in the Berkeley Public Library and the afternoons playing racketball in Golden Gate Park. But I wanted to tell my wife about it, to turn to her in bed, brush back her hair, and kiss her neck for a little noise before I began telling her what I had done two summers before. I wanted to tell her while we were in bed, with books and magazines. "Carolyn," I would begin, "sometimes do you think I'm a little crazy?" She would nod her head yes at her novel. She would smile at the pages and then lift her bright face, eyes like shiny triangles. If I told her, I would have to hold her in my arms and begin slowly with sailboats and freighters and the bay seen from a roof top before I placed an innocent but married man in an apartment with a worldly but single woman. Then she would catch on and her hug would turn into a squeeze that would hurt. Squeeze, squeeze, and the whole story would come out like toothpaste. A little crying, a little laughter. "You're a crazy one," she would say and during the coming nights, if not weeks, she would hug me and ask for more secrets. "Please, sweetheart," she would coo. If I said there

was none, she would squeeze until I had to make up
something with sailboats and freighters, and a man
and a woman who looked out to a body of water
that was bluer than what they remembered.

Money

SOMETIMES IT'S MONEY that I want. I open my passbook and see the numbers rise and fall from $2,300 to $850 to $1,200. The figures are black as rain that won't let up. Black, and more black. I'm amazed where it goes—the big chunks I mean—because when I look around the room there's nothing I can remember buying. The couch has been here for years, first as a cow and now as a place for my daughter to jump up and down . . . until she pops over the edge, head first and already crying. The table has been here for years. The chairs. The refrigerator. The bed was given to us for having a baby, and the dresser that's followed us from place to place like a good dog is cluttered with things that seem foreign: a hat, dolls, a basket of spools, and a school of black whales the size of thumbnails.

I look out the window: my car is a 1966 Chevy, blue as a piece of sky. The lawn is old, the trees, the walk pushed up by a stubborn root trying to make its way under the earth. On the side of the house, though, the hedge is gone. I remember spending money there. I hired a friend to pull it out, a burly black guy who, during lunchbreak, ate sandwiches and chips and played my guitar on the steps, to the amazement of an older couple who were holding down their hats as they walked to church.

I paid him one hundred and twenty dollars to rip out the hedge. I paid him forty dollars to haul pieces of concrete. He lugged them like typewriters, grunting when he threw them onto the bed of his truck. Another thirty went to hauling weeds. Another thirty went to pruning a tree that's now bare as a hatrack and perhaps just as fruitless. We'll just have to see in spring.

But that was not much money. Where had the rest gone? I know there's rent and groceries. Our daughter is now in school. Dresses smother her closet; books are staggered against the wall like ancient ruins. But she demands very little—literally. Little saucers, little skirts and little shoes. A big day for her is a handful of sand in a park or toy cars overturning in the grass. And there are her friends, girls with scuffed knees and running noses. But they are almost free, except for chocolates that invariably stain their dresses.

Maybe my wife is spending the money. She does have clothes with names I can't pronounce. Her shoes look like they're standing on tip toes—high heels the color of lipstick. She has a fur coat but she's worn it for years, even before our marriage. It's a thrift-shop coat with a rip in the armpit, so when our daughter and I point at airplanes or statues or bridges lit with cars, she just stands there with hands in her pockets, smiling but not joining in on the fun.

My wife hasn't made up her mind who she wants

to be. She seems to be spending money. A line of perfumes, like foreign soldiers, stands on the dresser. She taps a fragrance on her wrist and the back of her knee, and asks, "Guess who wears this kind?" When she opens up her drawer, scarves pop up like magic. When she opens one of her many lacquered boxes, cheap jewelry that's really expensive glows like crying eyes. There are, of course, the make-ups that blush and highlight and cover what should be seen. One day she looks girlish with the no-make-up look; another day she is the hard, MBA Asian, with eyebrows like hatchets.

I admit I spend money. I admit that I buy lunches (even when my wife packs me a lunch of a sandwich and an apple) at restaurants that serve food from countries that are barely on the map, like Ceylon and Liechtenstein. And I admit that I sometimes buy clothes I don't need—jackets and sports coats, shirts and Italian slacks with designer labels that can't be seen without getting intimate. The other day I was foolish, but not foolish enough to make myself look good. Alone, without my wife and her eyebrows raised into hatchets, I test drove a BMW through Oakland and into Piedmont, past two-story homes with feathery smoke rising from chimneys. At a quiet corner I idled the car, a smirk starting up in my soul, and then raced the car so that the leaves in the street seemed to fly. But in the end, I said I'd talk to my wife, shook the hand of the salesman who wouldn't let go even as I walked backwards, and got back into my Chevy for the drive home and a Sunday dinner.

Today it's money that I want, a deep green in my wallet when it yawns open at clothing stores. "Cash, sir?" asks the salesman whose own wallet is toothless, a piece of leather with no bite.

"Yes, this will be cash," I say and peel twenties into his outstretched hand. At a restaurant, when the check comes on a black tray, I pull out a wallet that growls for me to open up. I pay and pay some more when I got outside to buy flowers that do tricks to my eyes.

But who knows why I feel this way. Perhaps it is a stage in my life when money is happiness. I find this difficult to believe, though, because last week I said to my wife that we should be poor, really poor. If we looked out our front window, we would see hard dirt; if we looked around the living room, we would see lint scuttling like clouds across the floor. "It's really a rich life—being poor, honey," I said. She said "umm, ummm" into the mirror as she plucked her eyebrows into even fiercer hatchets, a towel wrapped into a turban around her washed hair and body still steaming from a jungly shower. I talked and talked as I dressed. My wife walked around my words and me as she prepared for dinner and a movie and, later in bed, said in a breathy voice, "What do you want more than anything in the world?" "I want you, right now"—I replied. "It's going to cost you, silly boy," and she squeezed me for all that counts.

This Man

IF I CLOSE MY EYES I see the ocean and my family walking slowly at its shore. A wheel of gulls spins noisily over the incoming waves and on a heaped garbage can a lone gull stands profiled, shifting its feet so that it turns to face us. My younger brother races to scare the gull, but stops when it doesn't leap skyward. He looks back at us. Wind is in his hair, in his smile, in his eyes that are almost squinted shut. He races back to us, a family on a weekend vacation to Pismo Beach, this family that is surprised to be there with the sea and the clouds and the sun almost breaking through.

I remember that weekend. My stepfather, home from work and two hours of whiskeys and beers at Uncle Tom's Cabin, sat drunkenly at the kitchen table babbling about how all he wanted was to lie on sand and think about nothing. You can leave me there, he said. Crushed beer cans piled up in front of his folded arms. His eyes floated in alcohol. His jowls were reddened into fleshy lamps. Just leave me there, he said all night, beer after half-finished beer, until we climbed into bed and tried to sleep.

Concrete. Kids. Warehouse work. He was a tired man when he came into my life—two years after my father's death—and even more tired when he spent days talking about the sea and the whip of wind in his face. He sat in his chair whose arms were slick from wear and oily forearms, the stench of vinegary sweat worked into the fabric. He sat hurting from the endless bend-and-pick-up of boxes he set on a conveyor belt. He hurt from the house payments, the asking wife, the five hungry kids to clothe and offer someday to the world.

He sometimes dreamed aloud with the television on, with a flash of too-much-drinking in his speech. While we did our homework in pajamas, we pretended to listen to his slurred echo of *leave me there, leave me there.* Later, in our bedroom we mimicked his dream, and bad mouthed his stench, his face, and his eyes that couldn't find the fork in his hand.

But his kids and wife worked into his dream. We all piled into our Rambler, drove the 150 miles from Fresno to Pismo Beach, and stayed at a run-down beachfront motel. We spent hours walking up and down the beach. Toward dusk we ate sandwiches in our room and watched the ocean fool around with small boats tied to the pier. Two times we went to an arcade where all seven of us watched others drop nickels and dimes into pinball machines, bowling games, and cranes that picked up plastic capsules of surprises. We were each given a quarter, which grew hot in our hands as we walked up and down looking for the best machine to play. I spent my first dime on bowling. The second dime went to racing a car. I wove in and out of traffic, sometimes slamming into the back end of other cars, and sometimes running red lights and riding up curbs to crash into buildings. I laughed at the mechanical flames but groaned when the game stopped suddenly. My sister and I pooled our nickels and played pinball while our brother Rick looked on . . . flipping his nickel into the air as he tried to break our concentration so that the final steel ball would roll quietly past our flippers.

An hour in the arcade, seven hours on the beach. We walked up and down, played tag with the waves, collected broken shells and rocks rich with color, and popped the slimy bulbs on the strings of kelp that littered the shore. Our mother and stepfather walked slowly behind, almost touching. They looked around, smoked cigarettes, and sometimes laughed when a wave licked their shoes wet.

Although it was a cold day, our stepfather did lie in the sand. He sent Rick back to the motel for a blanket. He shook it into the air but the wind tangled it. Rick and I helped him flatten the blanket and hold the corners down as he fixed himself onto it, face up. He closed his eyes, laced his fingers together on his chest, and told us to scram. Mother had already returned to the motel because of the cold. We watched him for a while but then ran up the beach to play keep-away with a soggy tennis ball. Later, my youngest brother and I sneaked back to watch him, our tired father, lie quiet as the dead. We crawled on our bellies until we were a few yards from him. He was very still, with grains of sand on his eyelids, wind flicking his hair out of place. This is what he wanted:

to lie on sand, to quiet his mind and think nothing of the ocean, his kids, or the work that would end when he ended. I closed my eyes and heard the slap of waves on water. I heard a gull. My brother. My sister yelling for the ball. I opened my eyes to see a man get his wish: to lie on sand, to be nowhere but in his flesh.

Finding a Wife

I'ʀ EASY TO find a wife, I told my students. Pick any-body, I said, and they chuckled and fidgeted in their chairs. I laughed a delayed laugh, feeling hearty and foolish as a pup among these young men who were in my house to talk poetry and books. We talked, occa-sionally making sense, and drank cup after cup of coffee until we were so wired we had to stand up and walk around the block to shake out our nerves.

When they left I tried to write a letter, grade pa-pers, and finally nap on the couch. My mind kept turning to how simple it is to find a wife; that we can easily say after a brief two- or three-week courtship, "I want to marry you."

When I was twenty, in college and living on a street that was a row of broken apartment buildings, my brother and I returned to our apartment from a game of racketball to sit in the living room and argue whether we should buy a quart of beer. We were college poor, living off the cheap blessings of rice, raisins, and eggs that I took from our mom's refriger-ator when Rick called her into the backyard about a missing sock from his laundry—a ploy from the start.

"Rick, I only got a dollar," I told him. He slapped his thigh and told me to wake up. It was almost the end of the month. And he was right. In two days our paychecks from Zak's Car Wash would burn like good report cards in our pockets. So I gave in. I took the fifteen cents—a dime and five pennies—he had plucked from the ashtray of loose change in his bedroom, and went downstairs, across the street and the two blocks to Scott's Liquor. While I was returning home, swinging the quart of beer like a lantern, I saw the Japanese woman who was my neighbor, cracking walnuts on her front porch. I walked slowly so that she looked up, smiling. I smiled, said hello, and continued walking to the rhythm of her hammer rising and falling.

In the apartment I opened the beer and raised it like a chalice before we measured it in glasses, each of us suspicious that the other would get more. I rattled sunflower seeds onto a plate, and we pinched fingersful, the beer in our hands cutting loose a curtain of bubbles. We were at a party with no music, no host, no girls. Our cat, Mensa, dawdled in, blinking from the dull smoke of a sleepy afternoon. She looked at us, and we looked at her. Rick flicked a seed at her and said, "That's what we need—a woman!"

I didn't say anything. I closed my eyes, legs shot out in a V from the couch, and thought of that girl on the porch, the rise and fall of her hammer, and the walnuts cracking open like hearts.

I got up and peeked from our two-story window that looked out onto a lawn and her apartment. No one. A wicker chair, potted plants, and a pile of old newspapers. I looked until she came out with a broom to clean up the shells. "Ah, my little witch," I thought, and raced my heart downstairs, but stopped short of her house because I didn't know what to say or do. I stayed behind the hedge that separated our yards and listened to her broom swish across the porch, then start up the walk to the curb. It was then that I started to walk casually from behind the hedge and, when she looked at me with a quick grin, I said a hearty hello and walked past her without stopping to talk. I made my way to the end of the block where I stood behind another hedge, feeling foolish. I should have said something. "Do you like walnuts," I could have said, or maybe, "Nice day to sweep, isn't it?"—anything that would have my mouth going.

I waited behind that hedge, troubled by my indecision. I started back up the street and found her bending over a potted geranium, a jar of cloudy water in her hand. Lucky guy, I thought, to be fed by her.

I smiled as I passed, and she smiled back. I returned to the apartment and my bedroom where I stared at my homework and occasionally looked out the window to see if she was busy on the porch. But she wasn't there. Only the wicker chair, the plants, the pile of newspapers.

The days passed, white as clouds. I passed her house so often that we began to talk, sit together on the porch, and eventually snack on sandwiches that were thick as Bibles, with tumblers of milk to wash down her baked sweet bread flecked with tiny crushed walnuts.

After the first time I ate at her house, I hurried to the apartment to brag about my lunch to my brother who was in the kitchen sprinkling raisins on his rice. Sandwiches, I screamed, milk, cold cuts, chocolate ice cream! I spoke about her cupboards, creaking like ships weighed down with a cargo of rich food, and about her, that woman who came up to my shoulder. I was in love and didn't know where to go from there.

As the weeks passed, still white as clouds, we saw more of each other. Then it happened. On another Saturday, after browsing at a thrift shop among gooseneck lamps and couches as jolly as fat men, we went to the west side of Fresno for Mexican food— menudo for me and burritos for her, with two beers clunked down on our table. When we finished eating and were ready to go, I wiped my mouth and plucked my sole five-dollar bill from my wallet as I walked to the cashier. It was all the big money I had. I paid and left the restaurant as if it were nothing, as if I spent such money every day. But inside I was thinking, "What am I going to do?"

Scared as I was, I took Carolyn's hand into mine as we walked to the car. I released it to open the door for her. We drove and drove, past thrift shops she longed to browse through, but I didn't want to stop because I was scared I would want to hold her hand again. After turning corners aimlessly, I drove back to her house where we sat together on the front porch, not touching. I was shivering, almost noticeably. But after a while, I did take her hand into mine and that space between us closed. We held hands, little tents opening and closing, and soon I nuzzled my face into her neck to find a place to kiss.

I married this one Carolyn Oda, a woman I found cracking walnuts on an afternoon. It was a chance meeting: I was walking past when she looked up to smile. It could have been somebody else, a girl drying persimmons on a line, or one hosing down her car, and I might have married another and been unhappy. But it was Carolyn, daughter of hard workers, whom I found cracking walnuts. She stirred them into dough that she shaped into loaves, baked in the oven, and set before me so that my mouth would keep talking in its search of the words to make me stay.

Moving Around

WE'RE GOING TO MOVE around until things look right, move left or right, into this house or that house, into a fancy car or no car at all. So it is with me and my wife, and now a daughter, a tiny reader who's jumping from picture book to picture book without so much as a word. And so it is with others who, like us, settle into one way of living only to get up and move into another.

If I look back I think of how we moved from car to car, most of which were no better than a faceful of smoke. My Buick Roadmaster limped up the streets like a hurt rhino; my $85 Rambler was ugly and died of ugliness on the way to the junk yard. My wife and I sold a perfectly good Volkswagen for a perfectly useless sportscar that gleamed in glossy photographs, beckoning us to be the happy couple leaning against it. It smoked badly, made noises, leaked puddles of oil in the driveway. The engine was so bad bicycles passed us up. Then there was another Volkswagen, then an Audi, then a Volkswagen convertible we still weep for that we traded for an Oldsmobile, which I gave to my in-laws after three years. I turned around and bought a 1966 Chevy that could pull your hair back, if not tears from your eyes, on a black stretch of highway.

We've moved from car to car, and house to house. Since we've been married—ten years—we've lived in twenty different places, two states, two countries, eight cities and five counties. We itch to get up and go, to keep the body and mind moving, to find ourselves before a window that brings in more light, or less light, or no light at all. And once we're settled into a new place, we begin work: old wallpaper comes down, the kitchen is painted and fitted with curtains over the sink, and patches of earth are turned over for a vegetable garden that, after so many hours of labor, offers only a handful of carrots, some gritty radishes, and anemic tomatoes that bleed in our palms. We eat and feel good, but only for a while.

We look forward to less tangible changes, like new seasons. Today, it's April 12, the beginning of baseball season and breezy picnics, and already I want it to be midsummer, a 41–23 season for the Giants, and the sun bullying people to flap their shirts in front of air conditioners. I want, however foolishly, for time to hurry up with its shadows, to make things new so that my eyes can keep taking in a vital world. If it's fall, I want it to be winter, and once it's winter I want it to be spring, and once it's spring I want a sun and its bonnet of heat over my head.

It's the same with love. A few days ago while on my way to work, I was thinking that it was possible to start up with another: a young woman was at the corner with her bicycle waiting for the light to turn green. I was waiting, too. I didn't want to go when the light changed, but instead wanted to pull my car to the side of the street, park, and go off with her for coffee that would grow cold without us so much as touching it. I wanted to say something tender and begin a love I could later remember over a beer with friends. Yesterday, though, it was a different matter: a young woman on a bicycle crossed against a red light without looking, so that I had to brake and send my books sailing into the dash. I honked and said bad words under my breath. "Damn women," I muttered and raced my redneck car all the way to work.

Mercurial. Fickle. Capricious. I admit I'm all three, and maybe more. I don't know why I can't settle down and not move—literally. Perhaps I'm exercising my migrant genes: to break camp and hit the road for another field, grape, or beet. Perhaps there's a dissatisfaction I swallow like spit each morning but won't admit: my wife is my love, my daughter is my love, and all that hurts from childhood is healed over. Is there more than this? Is there more than family and family's good-hearted friends? To understand me, and people like me, it would take a doctor or a wise man with a beard so long that whole cities could hold on to it and be saved.

I keep moving up the street, looking for the new. And once I'm where I think I should be, I sometimes mourn for the days that have come and gone: the cars, the houses, the young wife who ran to meet me in a flaring dress. I look forward to what lies ahead, and feel a sorrow for what collects in memory. I'm in between tomorrow and yesterday, a Friday lunch date and Wednesday night when my wife and I played with each other's hair, kissed, and made a happy love that came out even.

Listening Up

IF YOU LISTEN UP, you may hear something worth keeping, some scintillating phrase to turn over like a foreign coin and call your own.

One summer I heard our three-year-old daughter Mariko say, "The days are filled with air," and heard my writer self say, "That's mine. I said that." It was a busy Sunday at Tilden Park. Fathers were chasing balls. Kids were riding the backs of their mothers for gum, popcorn, snow cones, a hot quarter for a video game. Babies in strollers were drooling onto their hands, and dogs were prancing up and down grassy knolls in an utter happiness humans may never know. It was the kind of Sunday when a parent might want nothing more than to sit in bed with a newspaper as thick as a pillow, the blinds drawn, and the radio throwing out a tinny noise of violins. The day, and the day's shadows, would crawl by without you. The sun would look down over trees and fall so slowly westward that you would cheer the tagged-on hours you seemed to inherit by being alone.

But I wasn't in bed that day. I was among other families in Tilden Park, pulling my child here and there: the animal farm and the lake, the nature room and a tree-lined path that narrowed to a small river of leaves. Mariko kicked those leaves until she coughed and her eyes teared from the dust. I wiped her eyes and led her back to the car, and drove down the hill to the merry-go-round.

We stood in line, looked around, and then rushed to the growling lion, to the German music, to the spinning blur of people watching us go round and round with smiles big as hats—to her saying, "The days are filled with air."

When she said this, I leaned over her shoulder to ask her to say it once more. She looked up at me, hair lifting in the snappy breeze of the merry-go-round, and only smiled, not answering because she couldn't hear above the music. But I heard her: "The days are filled with air."

When the ride stopped, we got off and walked to an out-of-the-way knoll. I sat down with a grunt and opened our sack lunch. I couldn't stop looking at her as she worked her way through half a sandwich on her way to the cheese and avocado. Finally, I suggested that we talk about school and her friends or what she liked most of all in the whole world. She stared at me while chewing, swallowed, and rolled her tongue around in her mouth without answering. I coaxed her again, and she drank from her straw, cleared her throat, and finally said, "Your hair is a poodle, Daddy."

Little philosopher, sophist, wise-guy in a little girl's dress—she spoke a beautifully true line that suggests that the business of living (jobs, friends, love, failed love, and so on) is only air, and maybe not even blue air at that. All is transparent as air—a breeze here, a strong gust there, and people and days pass from our lives.

What magic from a watchful eye! I heard her make an observation that she herself was not fully aware of; it surfaced from one brain cell or another into her mouth and finally into my listening ear. This amazed me. We were spending a Sunday together. We were smiling in spring clothes like so many others when without warning she spoke a line of beauty, some truth to argue over all the way to the grave.

Probably other kids open their mouths to such turns of language—kids who themselves spin on merry-go-rounds with their half-asleep fathers holding the reins of wooden horses.

We're not listening or, if we are, we only smile and laugh at these cute spoken truths: perceptions that are more lush, more acute than the ones that issue from our mouths. They speak in clever ways, and we smile and touch their hair and let the words go, failing to remember what they say.

I took my daughter's line and made a poem from it. I gave this little one a hug. And an ice cream cone.

The Arts

I've always been amazed by what other people can do with watercolors and a sheet of paper because I've known for years that I wasn't meant for the arts. In first grade I drew a car and the teacher, a kind one with a warm hand, said, "Nice house, Gary." I drew houses and she declared, with her hands jumping to her breast, "Oh my, the Golden Hind!" I drew people whose faces looked like lopsided toasters, and dogs that resembled Tyrannosaurus Rex on a leash. The hats were clouds, and the clouds were bushes, and what looked like a length of fence was really my brother and sister holding hands.

I loved drawing nevertheless. I could see what I was doing. The fort was a fort, the people on horses were Indians, and the ones with rifles were soldiers. At my work bench I moved my crayon back and forth as I made this and that. I studied the drawing with my mouth half open in full admiration and then, very quietly at first, scribbled flames that picked up speed like a real fire.

The houses that looked like cars burned; the bushes that were clouds went up in flame. Hot fire poked around rich families, boats, and hungry dogs. While I drew I made the sound of a race car, even after the teacher shushed me with a finger pressed to her puckered mouth. I went silent but the car noise raced inside my head at a ferocious speed.

I've always admired the beauty of art because, in a way, it suggests the beauty in us, or, as Wallace Stevens put it, "the voice that is great within us." I've also enjoyed singing even though I couldn't sing to save a poodle's life. In kindergarten I sang "Banana Boat." A deep longing rose from my heart when I yelled "It's a day, it's a day, it's a DAY-O." The teacher would stop her piano to shush me with a finger pressed to her mouth while her eyes slowly widened, something that my mother did when she was angry and meant business.

I sang with gusto. Among a horseshoe of children who sat crosslegged on the floor, beaming good looks and washed faces, I sounded off with the conviction of a criminal. When we came to the end—the best part for me—I lowered my voice to a bass, bowed my head slightly, and raised my eyes as if to take a peek inside my frontal lobe.

I remember when our mothers came to open house at school. We kids, decked out in our best, sat on the floor in a horseshoe to sing "Red River Valley" to the mothers who stood with their coats on in the front of the class. The teacher blew into her harmonica for the right pitch and then hummed another pitch, which was the cue for us to hold hands. Some mothers touched their hearts.

I saw my mother look plain faced at me. I was happy, though. Mother's going to be proud. She's going to clap even before I'm finished. When we began I went along with the others, but toward the end I got carried away—"But remember the Red River Valley/and THE ONE WHO LOVES YOU SO TRUE!" The teacher, strumming her guitar, made her eyes big at me, and Mother, who was taking off her coat, mouthed silent words that meant trouble if I didn't knock it off.

After our presentation, the mothers viewed our art work that we kept in our cubby holes. Smiling almost demonically, Mother picked me up roughly from the floor, but became soft as we walked over to look at my art work that was kept in a folder that glittered with stuck-on stars that spelled my name. "Pretty, mi'jo," she said before she peeled open my scrapbook of people on fire, houses on fire, a dog whose furry face was black smoke. Page after page, she puzzled over my drawings, only to close it and walk over to the teacher who shrugged her shoulders and said, "Who knows?"

I was no good at drawing or singing, but I was pretty good at half-remembering. One morning our teacher, who always took off her bracelet, watch, and ring to fingerpaint with us in the morning, gave a scream at music time when she rested her hands on the piano keys. Her ring was not on her finger. She got up and frantically searched her desk, the tables, our lunch-boxes, before she turned to us—little kids on the floor—and asked if anyone of us had picked up her ring from her desk. The ring was pretty, she said, but it was naughty of us to take things without permission. None of us said a word. Some of the girls looked at the boys. I stared down at my shoes, which were new and black as cockroaches, and remembered playing with the ring at recess when all the kids were outside. But where was it now? I bit my lip, thought deeply, but failed to remember where I had left the ring.

When no one answered she lined us up to check our pockets, but stopped when the girls began to sob. Our teacher left the room sobbing, only to return, red-eyed and shaky, with our principal who shook a finger of threats at us, even when the girls and one sissy boy began to cry. But he couldn't pull it out of us—a diamond wedding ring. I looked down at my shoes, scared inside but stupid-faced and seemingly unworried.

They searched the rest of the morning—our pant pockets hung like tired tongues. They frisked our pant cuffs and stripped off our shoes, which they shook and tapped against their palms. Worry darkened the principal's face. He made us get on all fours to search the floor. We crawled on the floor—little girls were sobbing, tough boys were mooing like cows and having a great time.

Our teacher cried. The principal clicked his tongue in disgust. When school let out I played in the yard for a while and then walked home, supremely happy, with a fiery sailboat pinned to my shirt and singing "It's a day, it's a day, it's a DAY-O." And the ring? God knows.

The Jacket

MY CLOTHES have failed me. I remember the green coat that I wore in fifth and sixth grades when you either danced like a champ or pressed yourself against a greasy wall, bitter as a penny toward the happy couples.

When I needed a new jacket and my mother asked what kind I wanted, I described something like bikers wear: black leather and silver studs with enough belts to hold down a small town. We were in the kitchen, steam on the windows from her cooking. She listened so long while stirring dinner that I thought she understood for sure the kind I wanted. The next day when I got home from school, I discovered draped on my bedpost a jacket the color of day-old guacamole. I threw my books on the bed and approached the jacket slowly, as if it were a stranger whose hand I had to shake. I touched the vinyl sleeve, the collar, and peeked at the mustard-colored lining.

From the kitchen mother yelled that my jacket was in the closet. I closed the door to her voice and pulled at the rack of clothes in the closet, hoping the jacket on the bedpost wasn't for me but my mean brother. No luck. I gave up. From my bed, I stared at the jacket. I wanted to cry because it was so ugly and so big that I knew I'd have to wear it a long time. I was a small kid, thin as a young tree, and it would be years before I'd have a new one. I stared at the jacket, like an enemy, thinking bad things before I took off my old jacket whose sleeves climbed half-way to my elbow.

I put the big jacket on. I zipped it up and down several times, and rolled the cuffs up so they didn't cover my hands. I put my hands in the pockets and flapped the jacket like a bird's wings. I stood in front of the mirror, full face, then profile, and then looked over my shoulder as if someone had called me. I sat on the bed, stood against the bed, and combed my hair to see what I would look like doing something natural. I looked ugly. I threw it on my brother's bed and looked at it for a long time before I slipped it on and went out to the backyard, smiling a "thank you" to my mom as I passed her in the kitchen. With my hands in my pockets I kicked a ball against the fence, and then climbed it to sit looking into the alley. I hurled orange peels at the mouth of an open garbage can and when the peels were gone I watched the white puffs of my breath thin to nothing.

I jumped down, hands in my pockets, and in the backyard on my knees I teased my dog, Brownie, by swooping my arms while making bird calls. He jumped at me and missed. He jumped again and again, until a tooth sunk deep, ripping an L-shaped tear on my left sleeve. I pushed Brownie away to study the tear as I would a cut on my arm. There was no blood, only a few loose pieces of fuzz. Damn dog,

I thought, and pushed him away hard when he tried to bite again. I got up from my knees and went to my bedroom to sit with my jacket on my lap, with the lights out.

That was the first afternoon with my new jacket. The next day I wore it to sixth grade and got a D on a math quiz. During the morning recess Frankie T., the playground terrorist, pushed me to the ground and told me to stay there until recess was over. My best friend, Steve Negrete, ate an apple while looking at me, and the girls turned away to whisper on the monkey bars. The teachers were no help: they looked my way and talked about how foolish I looked in my new jacket. I saw their heads bob with laughter, their hands half-covering their mouths.

Even though it was cold, I took off the jacket during lunch and played kickball in a thin shirt, my arms feeling like braille from goose bumps. But when I returned to class I slipped the jacket on and shivered until I was warm. I sat on my hands, heating them up, while my teeth chattered like a cup of crooked dice. Finally warm, I slid out of the jacket but a few minutes later put it back on when the fire bell rang. We paraded out into the yard where we, the sixth graders, walked past all the other grades to stand against the back fence. Everybody saw me. Although they didn't say out loud, "Man, that's ugly," I heard the buzz-buzz of gossip and even laughter that I knew was meant for me.

And so I went, in my guacamole-colored jacket. So embarrassed, so hurt, I couldn't even do my homework. I received Cs on quizzes, and forgot the state capitals and the rivers of South America, our friendly neighbor. Even the girls who had been friendly blew away like loose flowers to follow the boys in neat jackets.

I wore that thing for three years until the sleeves grew short and my forearms stuck out like the necks of turtles. All during that time no love came to me— no little dark girl in a Sunday dress she wore on Monday. At lunchtime I stayed with the ugly boys who leaned against the chainlink fence and looked around with propellers of grass spinning in our mouths. We saw girls walk by alone, saw couples, hand in hand, their heads like bookends pressing air together. We saw them and spun our propellers so fast our faces were blurs.

I blame that jacket for those bad years. I blame my mother for her bad taste and her cheap ways. It was a sad time for the heart. With a friend I spent my sixth-grade year in a tree in the alley, waiting for something good to happen to me in that jacket, which had become the ugly brother who tagged along wherever I went. And it was about that time that I began to grow. My chest puffed up with muscle and, strangely, a few more ribs. Even my hands, those fleshy hammers, showed bravely through the cuffs, the fingers already hardening for the coming fights. But that L-shaped rip on the left sleeve got bigger, bits of stuffing coughed out from its wound after a hard day of play. I finally Scotch-taped it closed, but in rain or cold weather the tape peeled off like a scab and more stuffing fell out until that sleeve shriveled into a palsied arm. That winter the elbows began to crack and whole chunks of green began to fall off. I showed the cracks to my mother, who always seemed to be at the stove with steamed-up glasses, and she said that there were children in Mexico who would love that jacket. I told her that this was America and yelled that Debbie, my sister, didn't have a jacket like mine. I ran outside, ready to cry, and climbed the tree by the alley to think bad thoughts and watch my breath puff white and disappear.

But whole pieces still casually flew off my jacket when I played hard, read quietly, or took vicious spelling tests at school. When it became so spotted that my brother began to call me "camouflage," I flung it over the fence into the alley. Later, however, I swiped the jacket off the ground and went inside to drape it across my lap and mope.

I was called to dinner: steam silvered my mother's glasses as she said grace; my brother and sister with their heads bowed made ugly faces at their glasses of powdered milk. I gagged too, but eagerly ate big rips of buttered tortilla that held scooped up beans. Finished, I went outside with my jacket across my arm. It was a cold sky. The faces of clouds were piled up, hurting. I climbed the fence, jumping down with a grunt. I started up the alley and soon slipped into my jacket, that green ugly brother who breathed over my shoulder that day and ever since.

The Concert

ONCE IN MEXICO CITY and tired of its noise and rushed people, my wife and I flew to Oaxaca, a city known for its pottery, weavings, and the nearby ruins of Monte Alban and Mitla. We stayed in a hotel whose courtyard was sheltered by a huge skylight that let in a hazy, almost silver light. For two days we took buses to the ruins, bought Mexican toys, and walked from one end of the town to the other in search of out-of-the-way shops.

On our last night we went to hear the National Symphony. I bought low-priced tickets but when we tried to sit on the ground floor, a portly usher pointed us to the stairwell. We climbed to the next landing where another usher told us to keep climbing by rolling his eyes toward *el paraíso*—the gallery of cheap seats. We climbed two more flights, laughing that we were going to end up on the roof with the pigeons. An unsmiling usher handed us programs as we stepped to the door. We looked around, amazed at the gray, well-painted boxes that were our seats. There were no crushed velvet chairs with ornate wooden arms, no elegant men and women with perfect teeth. Most were Indians and campesinos, and a few university students holding hands, heads pressed together in love.

I led Carolyn to the boxes in the front row against the rail and together we looked far down where the others sat. Their rumblings rose like heat. They fanned themselves and smiled wide enough for us to see their teeth. We watched them until an old man touched my shoulder, said *con permiso,* and took small steps to get past me to the box on our left. When he sat down I smiled at him as I wanted to be friendly. But he didn't look at me. He took out a pair of glasses from his breast pocket. They were broken, taped together at the bridge. I looked away, embarrassed to see that he was poor, but stole a glance when the program began: I saw his coat, slack and full from wear, and his pants with oily spots. His shoes were rope sandals. His tie was short, like a withered arm. I watched his face in profile that showed a knot of tape protruding from his glasses; a profile that went unchanged as it looked down at the symphony.

I listened but felt little as the violins tugged and pulled and scratched through an hour of performance. When the music stopped and the conductor turned around, moon-faced and trying to hide his happiness by holding back a grin, I craned my neck over the rail and watched the *elegantes* applaud and smile at one another. We applauded, too, and looked around, smiling. We were busy with an excitement that lit our eyes. But while the *elegantes* got up to take drinks and stand in the foyer under torches, those around us leaned against the wall to smoke and talk in whispers. A group of young men played cards and, in a sudden win, laughed so hard that the usher came over to quiet them down.

We stayed for the second half—something by Haydn—but no matter how I tried to study the movements of musicians and conductor on his carpeted box, I couldn't help but look around the room at the Indians and campesinos whose faces, turned in profile in the half-lit shadows, held an instinctive awareness of the music. They would scratch a cheek or an elbow, speak quietly to one another, and sometimes squirm on the boxes. But most were attentive. It amazed me. I had never known the poor to appreciate such music, and I had lived among the poor since I was a child. These field laborers and rug weavers listened to music that was not part of their lives, music written to titillate the aristocrats who wanted so much to rise above the dirty faces of the poor. The poor sat on the fifth tier on painted boxes, bodies leaning in the direction of the music that couldn't arrive fast enough to meet their lives.

When the concert ended, the old man next to me stood up and asked for permission to pass. I pinched my knees together and Carolyn stood up. She sat back down and together, heads touching like lovers, we looked down to the first floor where the *elegantes* chatted with drinks and fluttery fans, and shook each other's hands as if celebrating their wealth.

After a while we got up and, with campesinos who were talking about a recently read book, descended the four flights to the ground.

Canary, Cat and Dog

AT TIMES THE DAYS are so quiet, so harmless, that I could welcome a canary into our home—a canary with its rusty squeak and its nervous shifting from perch to perch. I welcome this bird. It taps its tiny bell, gargles seed, and looks over its shoulder like a poet into a mirror. "Paco, here's my finger"—and it flutters its wings, makes noises, and pokes with its trumpet of a beak. His bite doesn't hurt, just stings like bad medicine.

If not a canary, then I welcome a cat who's a furry thing from a wet road. I want to come home from school to find an orange one licking its bristle brush of a paw at my doorstep, a cat that raises its three-cornered head and gives me a "what's-there-to-eat" look. I step inside, put down my books, and yank open the refrigerator, the white light coming on.

"Cheese," I say, "there's cheese and olives and meats—and milk for your goofy face."

I fix a plate for the cat and together we sit by the fireplace, yellow from a few fired-up sticks and rolled newspapers. I offer the day's events, but the cat doesn't look up, only bobs and weaves its head over each bite. If it looks up, it is to see that I keep my distance, keep my sneaky hand away from the drumstick.

If not a canary or cat, then I welcome a dog who can walk briskly and purposefully down any mean street. Black, brown, black and brown—it's all the same to me. I welcome a street dog, fur like a wet rake. A dog who has stared into garbage cans and sniffed what was best. When I was a kid I owned a lost dog for a day. That day we walked together in alleys to search trees for fruit and peek into trash bins where we found tuna cans licked clean as cats. If I pulled out a light bulb to rattle a made-up song, the dog with dancing feet yanked out a soup can. He gripped it between his paws and lapped it until his tongue got tired, if not bloody. He looked around with his twitching nose in the air. Birds crossed up the sky; smoke rode on the wind. He twitched his nose, then lowered it back into the can for a final lick.

Yesterday on campus while on the way to class, I saw a mangy dog who had eaten egg shells in his lifetime. He was crouched behind a bench, tongue hanging and breathing hard. He looked at me and I looked at him and we almost recognized one another. If he could have talked, he would have held my stare and said, "Get over here! I know who you are."

And if I were less smart, I would sit on the bench and let him, a remembering dog, sniff my hand. "You're Mexican," he says. "What are you doing here, guy?"

—"Teaching."

—"Teaching, my foot! Chasing free lunches is more like it, sucker."

"Quiet," I say, embarrassed that my past has come back like a lost child. "Someone will hear."

Students. Professors with tenure votes. Young women in dresses like skimpy clouds. I look around, scared as a dunked cat, and tell him that things have changed—that I am an assistant professor, that I am reading almost great books, that I am thinking about Europe for the summer.

"You ain't thinking a damn thing," the dog says. He rises to his feet, stiffly. "I know who you are, so listen up."

And I do. I take his order: a sandwich, make that two, and a length of bologna still in its plastic wrapper. And water. And a flea collar. And dog eyedrops if they have them because he's been up all night looking for a good time. I go and come back because he's my kin, blood brother to bad days.

If he were smarter, and I less smart, there would be no choice. The alleys would call—the rich harvest of everything discarded and rank in the sun—and I would have to go because we are friends to the same past that won't lie down and die for good.

The Young Poet Under a Tree

LARRY WAS a college friend who lived under a tree. I would see him on campus with a book thin as a sandwich in his hand, or walking to a busy corner to hitchhike God knows where. He took me to his tree one day and together, on weeds flattened into a dusty carpet, we sat and talked, mostly about books we had read—Rimbaud and Hamsun—and sometimes about our poetry. I recall a poem of his about an Egyptian cat whose eyes were many-cornered diamonds. After a while he poured me a cup of water and measured a handful of seeds into my palms. They were unsalted, bland as paper, but I popped them into my mouth, one by one, while I talked about important books and the poems I wanted to write.

When our conversation stalled I got up and said that I had to leave. He got up also, asking me to wait because he wanted to give me something. When he turned his back, I looked around: his sleeping bag was rolled loosely and propped against the tree; a cardboard box showed cans of soup and tuna; a desk, with a scatter of fallen leaves, stood in sunlight. Larry hovered over it as he felt inside a drawer. He turned to me with a sheaf of lined paper—poems, I realized. He gave them to me to read, to have.

I left thinking how sad it was not to live in a house, and walked to my girlfriend's apartment, which was not more than twenty yards from the tree. Carolyn was on the front porch watering her spring plants from a milk carton. Yellow things yawned their brightness; carnations were nodding their ruffled heads in the noontime breeze. When I called to her, she looked up with a flash of happiness in her eyes. She hugged me with one arm, that first love of three weeks, and led me inside her apartment to make me a sandwich that I nibbled, fish-like, until it was only crumbs on a paper plate. After I finished a bowl of ice cream, we went outside, arm in arm, to sit on the front steps. But startled, I got up as I remembered Larry's poems. I went inside and returned to read them to Carolyn—poems about ancient learning, Greece, astrological signs. None of them made sense, though neither one of us let on that we didn't understand them. "He's very ambitious," I finally said after minutes of silence. Carolyn nodded her head. She took the poems and placed them face down, then asked me who had written them. I took her by the hand and led her to the back of her apartment where I pointed to a cluster of trees: feathery smoke and faint guitar-playing in the air.

"There's nothing over there," she said. Shushing her, I said that Larry the poet lived under a tree. She furrowed her brow and clicked her tongue, calling me "silly lover boy." She let go my hand and walked toward the tree to see for herself only to return, head down and troubled as she hurried back to her apartment where she threw herself on the bed and told me to go home. I cooed words into her ear, petting her hair and massaging her shoulders as I tried to perk her up. Not knowing what to do, I told her, however lamely, that someone had to be poor. I bit the back of my hand, realizing how stupid it sounded, and got off the bed to look out the window: smoke rose not in a feathery column but in huge, cheeky puffs. His guitar was noisier, his southern voice was louder. I imagined him sitting on a box while his big shoe tapped quietly to his playing. The poor were so close, so real, that you could close your eyes and see them anytime.

The Man on the Floor

YESTERDAY MORNING my wife and I worked up the ground for spring planting. This was something new for us—a garden we could see from the kitchen window. Ferns and begonias would go along the fence and, farther back, near the fig tree where there was more sun, would grow tomatoes, chiles, and maybe eggplant, those lopsided heads I disliked as a kid but love now.

While I shoveled, my wife shook out grassy roots and wild onion that she piled like wet laundry. At first we worked talking about our new house: how we would panel the bathroom with redwood and put in a greenhouse window. But as the rhythm of shovel-and-pull sped up, we worked quietly side by side, bent over and occasionally grunting from fatigue or a tough root. And even though it was cold, the sun gleamed behind clouds. Sweat moistened my face from the push and tug of shovel work. I wanted to take off my flannel shirt, but my wife said that I would catch cold. Even our daughter, who was waist high in a pile of leaves, was warm, her face pink from sucking a thumb. She raised many leaves to us, and each time we had to act surprised and open our mouths wide to say "Wow!"

We shoveled and pulled and leveled the ground with a rake. Afterwards we went inside to rest. But I couldn't stay. I had a meeting with students at 12:30. I drove and parked off campus, near Telegraph Avenue, and since I was early I went to Giant Hamburger to get something to eat. I was in line thinking about the garden when the man in front of me slugged the waitress who was taking his order. The blow pushed her back against the Coke machine, and a bright string of blood spilled from her mouth to her apron. My mind is not working, I thought. This can't be happening.

I saw the man's face twist with ugliness. I heard him yell, "You white bitch," and saw him pick up a pot of coffee. I heard myself think, "Grab him," and I did, in a sort of bear hug. He let go of the pot and, as he tried to wrestle free from my hold, I picked him up, pushed my weight on his, and together we went down to the floor—a high-school wrestling move that was more instinct than thought.

I took him down and used my weight, my chin in his back, an occasional head slap, to keep him down as one of the workers called the police. But he was strong and crawled, snail-like, calling, "You white mutherfucker, I'm going to kill you!" He said it repeatedly with such rage that I began to believe him, especially when, in spite of my hold, he started to rise to his knees. I pounded one of his arms from under him, so that he collapsed like a table. He shouted names, and I shouted back, "Mutherfucker, you ain't going to do shit!" I shouted until I was in a rage, like a chain saw dropped on the ground and dancing with fury. I hit him in the face, in the back, in the face again and even spat at him.

When he started to get up again, I looked to the customers who remained in the restaurant, some of whom were munching hamburgers and lapping up chips. "You guys better help me if this guy gets up," I said in a desperate voice, because I knew I was in trouble if he should reverse holds. But they looked at me dully and unmoved, and I was scared. I could hear the waitress sob and a worker talking to his boss on the phone. Another stood with a towel over his shoulder. I looked at him and he looked at me. Everything seemed heightened, like a movie seen too close to the screen.

What amazed me is that some people came into the restaurant but seeing us on the ground immediately turned to flee. There were those who came in, looked down at us as they walked to the counter, and tried to place an order, as if this were a common occurrence, as if Mexicans and black men often wrestle in restaurants.

When the police arrived, I let go and moved away so the black man wouldn't see my face. I didn't want him to know who I was or what color I was. I went into the back room where the waitress was sitting on a keg of beer, eyes still red from crying. She thanked me and I said it was nothing. She got up and from her jeans pulled out coupons for free hamburgers. "Come in anytime, and you order what you want," she offered. When a cop came in with a clipboard, I left the back room to a "thank you." She smiled and her teeth were fringed with blood.

I was leaving when one of the workers handed me a bag of burgers and fries, and another bag of Cokes. I thanked him and walked up the street a little tense, a little shaky, but only a half hour late to my meeting.

left the work scene to sit inside Alice of all and the friendly noodle bowl we had then.

To Be a Man

HOW STRANGE IT IS to consider the dishevelled man sprawled out against a store front with the rustling noise of newspaper in his lap. Although we see him from our cars and say "poor guy," we keep speeding toward jobs, careers, and people who will open our wallets, however wide, to stuff them with money.

I wanted to be that man when I was a kid of ten or so, and told Mother how I wanted my life. She stood at the stove staring down at me, eyes narrowed, and said I didn't know what I was talking about. She buttered a tortilla, rolled it fat as a telescope, and told me to eat it outside. While I tore into my before-dinner snack, I shook my head at my mother because I knew what it was all about. Earlier in the week (and the week before), I had pulled a lawn mower, block after block, in search of work. I earned a few quarters, but more often screen doors slapped shut with an "I'm sorry," or milky stares scared me to the next house.

I pulled my lawn mower into the housing projects that were a block from where we lived. A heavy woman, with veined legs and jowls like a fat purse, said, "Boy, you in the wrong place. We poor here."

It struck me like a ball. They were poor, but I

didn't even recognize them. I left the projects and tried houses with little luck, and began to wonder if they too housed the poor. If they did, I thought, then where were the rich? I walked for blocks, asking at messy houses until I was so far from home I was lost.

That day I decided to become a hobo. If it was that difficult pulling quarters from a closed hand, it would be even more difficult plucking dollars from greedy pockets. I wanted to give up, to be a nobody in thrown-away clothes, because it was too much work to be a man. I looked at my stepfather who was beaten from work, from the seventeen years that he hunched over a conveyor belt, stuffing boxes with paperback books that ran down the belt quick as rats. Home from work, he sat in his oily chair with his eyes unmoved by television, by the kids, by his wife in the kitchen beating a round steak with a mallet. He sat dazed by hard labor and bitterness yellowed his face. If his hands could have spoken to him, they would have asked to die. They were tired, bleeding like hearts from the inside.

I couldn't do the same: work like a man. I knew I had the strength to wake from an alley, walk, and eat little. I knew I could give away the life that the television asked me to believe in, and live on fruit trees and the watery soup of the Mission.

But my ambition—that little screen in the mind with good movies—projected me as a priest, then a baseball coach, then a priest again, until here I am now raking a cracker across a cheesy dip at a faculty cocktail party. I'm looking the part and living well—

the car, the house, and the suits in the closet. Some days this is where I want to be. On other days I want out, such as the day I was in a committee meeting among PhDs. In an odd moment I saw them as pieces of talking meat and, like meat we pick up to examine closely at supermarkets, they were soulless, dead, and fixed with marked prices. I watched their mouths move up and down with busy words that did not connect. As they finished mouthing one sentence to start on another, they just made up words removed from their feelings.

It's been twenty years since I went door to door. Now I am living this other life that seems a dream. How did I get here? What line on my palm arched into a small fortune? I sit before students, before grade books, before other professors talking about books they've yet to write, so surprised that I'm far from that man on the sidewalk, but not so far that he couldn't wake up one day, walk a few pissy steps saying, "It's time," and embrace me for life.

Going Back

MY WIFE AND I are devoted to Masterpiece Theatre, which is about the only television we watch, except for the best boxing matches and an occasional football game. We look forward to Sunday, nine o'clock, and the television throwing out its blue light and a good story; we look forward to hurrying Mariko to bed where she'll read for fifteen minutes before my wife and she say a pagan-style goodnight chant:

Sotooda Odooda
Podewda codewda
AHOOH Permew
Peacock Penguin
Pegasus Unicorn Butterfly
Stubby, the best and only goat we know.

Sunday night offers a little silence, a little solitude, a time away from our daughter. And like so many other parents, we enjoy an hour to ourselves, an hour in which the telephone is unplugged, the child is asleep, the half-written letters are put aside, and the demands of the house are unanswered—the sagging roof, the wood rot in the windows, the mystery of the water heater that snaps and rumbles when the toilet is flushed.

We crawl into bed, pillows propped up behind us, with one lamp making shadows that seem exciting. Then Alistair Cooke appears, cross-legged and elegant, one hand touching his brilliant, silver-streaked hair as he wets his lips and says, "Good evening. Tonight we're in the fourth episode that takes us . . ." And we're off, witnessing Claudius' stutter, Poldark's manly dismount from a horse, Lilly's glitter from champagne and jewels like tears on her breast.

It's not wholly the drama that keeps us sitting before the television, Sunday after Sunday, as it is the ritual of my wife and me being together, almost touching, almost tender, even with our hands that are greasy from popcorn. Now and then I will look at her, and she will squint her eyes, lovingly. Now and then she will rub my thigh and I'll move it closer until I'm almost sitting in her lap. It's a happy hour that is seldom long enough.

The second time I held my wife's hand was at the movie *Sounder,* on March 19, 1973. I remember that date because I wrote it so many times in my notebook that I can't forget it.

That night at the movie my hand crawled like a dizzy crab into her hand, which she snapped up to my surprise. I looked at the screen for two hours, oblivious to what was going on. I couldn't throw my heart out to the characters of a story that didn't make any sense. Love-struck, my heart made noises under my shirt and sweater. I held her hand without looking at her, though occasionally I stole a quick glance at her hand that was over mine.

Later, I put my arm around her shoulder as we walked to the car and, still later, at my apartment, I snuggled my face into her neck and kissed and kissed until she was saying, "No, Gary, please no," which meant, according to my older brother, "Yes, yes, please!" I stopped, however, and offered Carolyn a bowl of ice cream, which she ate heartily. To keep her there longer, I offered another bowl, but she declined. Placing the bowl on the coffee table, she shivered from the cold, a perfect cue for me, and I leaned against her, my face again meeting hers. I said soft words; I brushed her hair from her eyes and outlined her brow with a finger. I played with a button, then another, until she was again saying, "No, Gary, please no," which of course meant yes to about everything.

So it still goes, thirteen years later. It began in a theater and continues on Sunday nights with Masterpiece Theatre. That is, it continues if we can get Mariko to sleep, a child who is very good but already a ferocious reader who likes to stay up. A month ago we let her read in bed for half an hour before we turned the lights out. Thinking she was asleep, I sneaked into the kitchen to make popcorn and lemonade. When I started back to the bedroom with two tumblers pinched in one hand and a bowl in the other, I heard Mariko call from her bedroom, "What are you doing?"

Caught like a rat, I looked at her in the semi-dark, "Mom and Dad are going to watch their program." I looked at her and she at me, knowing that that wasn't what she wanted to hear. I glanced down at the lemonade and popcorn. "And we're going to have a little snack."

At first she didn't say anything but only looked at me with mournful eyes. Then she said, "Sounds like you're going to have a wonderful time."

"Lie down, pumpkin," I said, lamely. I opened our bedroom door and Carolyn, who had already turned on the television, beamed a smile as I entered. I put down the tumblers and bowl on the side of the bed and knelt to tell Carolyn what Mariko had said.

"Oh, poor baby," she said sadly. "She's such a good girl."

"Let me get her," I suggested. I got up and carried her back as if she were flying, arms out like Wonder Woman's. She crashed into the pillow, utterly happy to be with us, to sit between us tossing popcorn into her mouth, big as a moon.

First Love

TO KNOW YOU'RE IN LOVE you have to step outside, walk up the street, and be so alone, so flogged by your separation, that your mind will race your heart and almost win. I did this one fall when I was twenty and so dazed by the separation from my girlfriend, who was on vacation, that I thumbed her photo in my room, confessing my one lust for another woman. Guilt caught like a chicken bone in my throat. I paced the room. I looked out the window. Yellow grass. Scraggly vines. Noisy sparrows in trees that were so thin that nothing could hide behind them.

I was rooming with my brother and two artist friends: one painted monkeys reading books in different places—subways and over-stuffed chairs—and the other shaped and pressed clay into elephant feet which he sold as ashtrays. My brother, an artist also, airbrushed eggs and red balls in the blue of untraveled space. In other words, the household was crazy. I couldn't turn to any one of them, open a beer and spill out my story. Instead I put on my coat, went downstairs and, looking left, looking right, went back upstairs to drag down my bicycle. I started off slowly in high gear, but to keep from thinking of

Carolyn, I rode faster. I passed City College and busy intersections into the residential streets with names like Poplar and Pine. Leaves shattered beneath my wheel and I loved the sound. I rode slowly admiring the lawns, the children puffed up in down jackets, and the feathery smoke of chimneys. The October sun was behind an overcast sky, almost breaking through, almost making shadows where there was only gray.

I stopped at a pharmacy in the Tower District and read magazines until the cashier, a woman with blue hair, adjusted her glasses so often that I finally got the message. I bought a candy and, to keep from thinking of Carolyn, I immediately picked up my bike and rode so fast that things looked blurry and confused my eyes. I pedaled in the direction of the canal where I and Benny Jeung, a friend of many years, had ridden inner tubes through languid days of our best summers. I stopped my bike. I stood at the water's edge to look down at the dark water of leaves and sticks. I sat on the weedy bank tossing rocks, and thought of Carolyn and what she might be doing in Canada on her vacation. It must be like here, I thought. Lots of leaves. Cold sky. Few people going about. I blew out a puff of white breath, and thought she might be doing the same by some river, quick with salmon. I saw her in a sleeping bag, the lantern at her side throwing out an aura of heat and light. She was writing postcards, one after another. She brushed back her hair that kept falling into her eyes as she hurried little messages to her family and her new lover, me. Growing sad, I got up and started off again because I didn't want to think about her. I rode to the Fresno Mall where I bought a bag of popcorn at Woolworth's, and walked up and down the aisles that glittered with toys, pans . . . and record albums at half-price. From there I went to Gottschalks where I dreamed of new clothes, bright Kensington shirts and stiff Levi's.

I rode to South Fresno, the place of my birth, and in an abandoned house on Sarah Street searched closets where I found overcoats, vests, and shoes seeming to sleep on their sides. On the back porch sat a stack of newspapers, musty stories from the fifties. What a find, I glowed, and carried an armful back to the apartment where, with my roommates who put down their brushes, I sat on the floor reading about deaths and weddings and housing tracts going up not far from where we lived. The four of us said very little as we bit our lips and read with knitted brows while the newspapers made a dull rustle in our hands when we turned the pages, fanning a musty smell into the air.

But after a while my roommates got up, one by one, and went back to their art. I sat alone with a pile of newspapers, with their stories and ads and brown photographs of women in dresses like frilly lampshades. When the cat nudged my leg, I thought of Carolyn who was probably reading a newspaper in Canada. She was in the lobby of her hotel, leg wagging as she waited for her friend to come back from making a telephone call in the bar. Again growing sad, I folded the newspapers and put them out onto the balcony. When I came back in, when I couldn't think of anything to do, I gave up and went to my bedroom to indulge, to hover over the photograph of my girlfriend standing by a tree, smiling. Beautiful, I smiled back. I looked out the window and things were beginning to disappear in the dusk.

All day I had tried to keep my mind from thinking of her, this first love. Ride a bicycle. Pick up things, put things down. Talk with my brother, with my roommates. Feed the cat fourteen times. Now I was alone, willing to surrender myself to a deep longing. To do it right, to think of the woman who mattered in my life, I put on my jacket and went downstairs again, but instead of taking my bicycle I walked up the street that got longer with each step. The farther I got from my apartment, the clearer the picture of her became, so that after a few blocks I was talking, almost singing, as if she were right next to me, her feet moving a little quicker to my longer strides, but keeping up so that we could be together for that walk and others.

This Is Who We Are

THIS PAST DECEMBER while on my way to Fresno for Christmas, I picked up two hitchhikers in Modesto. Usually I won't stop; usually I only have time to glance at a sleeve or a blackened knee or a creased face, not the whole man, before I press the gas pedal to get the car going faster. Call it guilt, call it common sense—a quick knife along the throat could end all dreams. Still, when I see someone on the side of the road, I press the pedal and turn up the radio so my guilt can't hear itself.

In the early seventies, when I was a college student, I hitchhiked up and down California, especially Highway 99, that black snake that runs through the valley—Sacramento, Modesto, Turlock, Madera, Fresno, Tulare, Delano, and Bakersfield. I kicked cans along my way, hid behind cows when the police crept on frontage roads, and felt so cut off from school and family that I was another person. Only in Strathmore, a trucker going a different way let me off. I thanked him, shrugging my backpack onto my shoulder, and for ten miles walked without caring if I flagged down a ride. The openness fascinated me. The sky, with a flap of geese angling south, was ash-color. Sparrows bickered on wire fences; cattle looked dully at the ground, drooling. The fields were brown in front of me but gray-black in the distance where the coastal range began. I walked in wonder at the quiet, at the absence of people, their voices and all their whining. I wondered at how simple it would be to lie in the grass and stay there until I looked like the grass—green, wet, and part of the world. But I went on and, by nightfall, I was in San Luis Obispo eating hamburgers with a friend in a makeshift tent.

I recall hitchhiking with others from Newhall, a suburb outside the San Fernando Valley, and being grateful that a truck had stopped, that the driver was human enough to recognize we were freezing among islands of snow turning to slush under the rain. There were five of us at the freeway entrance but room for only three in the cab. With another, I volunteered to get in the bed of the truck. I had been cold on the side of the road but was colder as the truck climbed the mountains on the way to Tehachapi and the quick descent into the Central Valley. Wind whipped our faces, making us shudder and beg the driver to pull over and let us ride in the cab for a while. But the driver, a grandfather in a plaid hunting jacket, didn't bother to look over his shoulder to see how we were doing. He was talking with everything he had—mouth, hands, brow that went up and down with lines—to the three in the cab, who were nodding their heads in agreement to whatever he was saying. When we finally stopped to let off two in Bakersfield, I was stiff from the rain and my hands were red, as if a flashlight were shining from behind them. I and the other person in the back hopped into the cab, thankful for the bell of warmth from the heater. The driver smiled at us; his eyes were glassy as if he had been drinking. He shifted gears and soon we were speeding past McFarland, Pixley, Delano, and the small towns of hard labor. He talked about Jesus and the sins of the world. Near Fowler the grandfather said that we hitchhikers could kill him and he wouldn't care. Jesus was on his side. Jesus would know everything. I hunched in my coat, occasionally peeking at the grandfather who wouldn't stop. I nodded my head to his talk and counted the miles to Fresno. This was a crazy man behind the wheel, a highway evangelist with us as his followers. We didn't bother to tell him to shut up even though he was a madman because we were grateful that he had saved us from the cold.

That was ten years ago when I was twenty-one. Last December I picked up two hitchhikers: one was, as he said, a bum, and the other was a private in the Army Reserve. The soldier, who was out of uniform, had come from a town outside Seattle hoping to reach El Paso by Christmas. He was broke, or nearly broke. When he had been discharged from basic training a month before, he took a bus to his hometown where he, a proud eighteen-year-old man, gave his mother $300. She bought groceries and booze, and after they were gone she told him to get a job. When he couldn't find one, she told him to get out. He left with bad words. Two days later he was in

California, in my car with a bum and a college professor who was failing at tenure.

And the bum? He was shivering when I picked him up, not from the cold but from a fever. He had spent the night at the freeway entrance, praying in the dark that someone would stop. But no one did. He was too ragged to trust. His face was a smear of dirty Vaseline; his coat was coming apart at the sleeves. When he got in, I could smell the stink of his unwashed clothes. The private could smell him too. But we pretended everything was OK, that he didn't have a fever and that he wasn't as poor as you can get without dying. I offered the two oranges and a sandwich, which they tore in half, thanking me three or four times. At first few words were exchanged, perhaps because they were tired or perhaps we didn't know how to begin. But by the time we were coming into Turlock, the bum was telling stories, from the easy days in Oklahoma City where he had worked as a bricklayer and had a house and family, to the bad year in San Quentin because he had "messed up" a friend for stealing his television.

"I just went crazy," he said. "I found him and beat him with a clock, an iron one. Looked like a wagon wheel."

He then quieted without telling us what had happened to him afterwards. He stared out the window to the fields that ran along Highway 99. A few minutes later, he was telling us how he and a buddy were jailed in a town outside Redlands in Southern California. They had been driving from Pomona to Needles in search of work and, tired from not sleeping the night before, had pulled to the side of the road to curl up for a couple of hours.

"It was hot, so I took off my shirt and shoes," he said. "And we were just sleeping when a cop was looking at us and saying we were drunk. But we weren't. We didn't have money to buy nothing."

He was arrested and released an hour later, though his friend remained jailed. When he asked for his shirt and shoes, the policeman pushed him out the door into the daylight that had the bum squinting like a criminal. The policeman went around the back of the police department and returned with a piece of cardboard the size of a surfboard. "These are your shoes, Okie," he said, flinging it at him. "Get your ass moving. Move!"

The bum described how it was so hot—110 degrees or hotter—that he couldn't take more than a dozen steps before he had to drop the cardboard and step on it, feet stinging like a hard slap. For two miles to the freeway, he ran, dropped the cardboard, and stood there until his feet cooled. He did it over and over. He did it while kids jeered on bicycles; while teenagers spit from their daddies' cars; while families in station wagons flicked balled ice cream wrappers at him. At the freeway entrance, he hunkered all afternoon, hurting for water and a cool place to sit as he waited for a car that finally stopped, eighteen hours later. The driver, a rancher from Oxnard, bought him burgers and Cokes, and in Redlands let him pick out shoes and a shirt at a thrift shop. He gave him two dollars and was gone.

He told other stories until I couldn't stand them and opened my own mouth to keep from hearing any more. I looked at him as I talked. His face—his eyes, his teeth—was used. He was shaking like a struck dog, this man with no luck to save himself. His life was over but the flesh went on, with the little memories of hope. I looked at the private in the rear-view mirror and he looked at me with eyes the color of river rock. He knew, I knew—this man was hurting. There was nothing we could do for him.

I pulled off in Madera to let the bum off. He thanked me without looking at me and trotted across a plot of freeway ivy toward an intersection. The private hopped in the front seat and for thirty miles to Fresno we said very little. He stared at the fields and commercial buildings—tire shops and farm equipment—in search of something to keep his mind busy. I was thinking of the words that had stung me. "The poorer you get, the more people think you look dead. And dead people don't need a damn thing."

I let the private off at a gas station in Fresno and drove to my in-laws for Christmas dinner, hoping that it wasn't true: the poor are like the dead, with little air space and no room to move.

One Thing After Another

ON DAYS when the mind wakes up it's possible to see that very little connects or can be reasoned out, like checkers or a quick hand of poker. Very little makes sense, especially in our lives. This seems curious. Last night, for instance, I was reading Montaigne, not in bunches, but in single paragraphs and sentences for he sometimes is a burden and goes on and on when he should be quiet. One idea leapt up in my mind and stayed there, like a blue flame.

We do not correct the man we hang; we correct others through him. I do the same. I relished the seemingly comic posture: Montaigne on a scaffold with his hair full of eager wind and some poor guy on his knees, a slack halo of rope descending over his bowed head. Then I read the idea as a bit of spoken wisdom and liked it even more: that through punishment of one guy we scare the hell out of other guys.

I read this master last night. This morning I got up and ran my index finger down the classified ads in search of a Pontiac Grand Prix, something with a tilt steering wheel and cruise control. I found a 1982 for $7,000, and drove to the suburban town of San Pablo where, at Accurate's body and fender, I sat tilting the wheel up and down. I adjusted the seat and the mirror that showed a piece of the sky. I checked the seats for tears or oily stains. A fender man in overalls came over and raised the hood. I pulled out the dip stick and plucked the belts and stared at the engine as if some oily part was going to do magic.

OK, now how did I get from reading a great essayist to wanting to buy a car. What brain cell said, "Pontiac"? What brain cell said, "Let's read, Gary"? I'm not sure. And I'm not sure why later that afternoon after this business with the car, I spent a half an hour with a secretary talking about Puerto Rico and still later I hurried over to a luncheon honoring Paul S. Taylor, a Professor Emeritus at Berkeley, who is, in spite of his Anglican birth, the first Chicano historian, or so I would like to think of him. He's a remarkable man, and a sad one, for he is nearing ninety and is in ill health: his arms are thin, his skin blotched, his eyelids held open with Scotch tape. When he talks you have to tilt an ear in the direction of a weak voice. We felt for this man, our first Chicano scholar, when he said over and over that he was happy to be presented a plaque. Tired, halfsmiling, he held it up with two hands for us to see. The bronze plaque winked a flashing light and then went dark when he laid it in his lap.

From there I returned home troubled because it hurt to see a man in his failing years. When it is all over, is this who we become? A man with a plaque, with Scotch tape holding open the eyes just a little more of the world? I gave my wife a hug, called my daughter "knucklehead," and went outside to the garage-turned-study until dinner time.

After dinner I lay on the couch, belly full and groaning when my daughter, a play doctor, gave me a shot in the head and asked if I felt better. I said yes. She lined her brow, looking worried as a real doctor, and said there were tiny holes on my nose. She gave me a shot for every hole and two long ones for my nostrils.

I got up with a start before she had finished my treatment when I remembered that the Mancini-Chacon fight was that night. If I can read Montaigne, mull over a car, and praise a great man all in less than 24 hours, then why not see the fight of the year? It was as good an entertainment as anything I could think of for the night. I called to Carolyn who was finishing the dishes to get dressed because we were going to see the fight. A light came on in her eyes as she hurried to the bedroom to dress and remake her face for the evening. I drove our daughter to my sister's place—my sister, a fight fan from the year one, pounded a fist into her palm and wished Chacon all the luck. When I returned home Carolyn was sitting cross-legged on the couch in her thrift shop fur, waiting.

We drove to the Ivy Room in Albany, a bar with cable television. When we walked in the patrons on barstools looked up from their drinks to show us veined noses and eyes like red scribbling. They looked tired and heavy in their heavy coats. Biker types were playing shuffleboard, whooping it up when one knocked the other's puck over the edge. The bartender, with his shirt sleeves rolled up, dipped glasses into soapy water, shook them until he thought they were clean, and then immersed them in clear water. We took a seat near the television, which was on with the sound turned down, ordered a beer for myself and a Calistoga for Carolyn, and talked about our recently purchased house, money, family, and our daughter the would-be doctor, as we waited for the fight to start. We then went quiet, looking around. It was a strange place, this redneck bar. I snuggled my face into her neck and asked if she was having fun. She raised her eyebrows and said, "You sure know how to treat a girl to a swell time." She took a long and hard swig of her Calistoga as she looked at me with eyes big as they could get.

When the fight started, two heavy guys moved their beers and themselves closer to the television. One looked drunkenly at Carolyn as he passed and sat down with a grunt in his chair. He looked up in silence at the screen. "Ching chong," he then started in. "Let's get some ching chong food." He turned to his friend. "What do you say, Dickie babe?" His friend, whose eyes were on the television and the first round that had Chacon against the ropes, said, "What the hell are you talkin' about?"

"Ching Chong food."

His friend turned stiffly to him. "You're a crazy gook."

I was uneasy by their talk. Knowing Carolyn was Asian, they were being insulting and largely stupid. I tried to ignore them as it was the second round and Chacon was against the ropes again, gloves up and sliding away from Mancini's pitbull tenacity. But the heavy guys continued with the made-up words of "Chow Wow Bow Wow" and "Ching Ga Ge Cho Cho." I'd had enough. I started with an Okie drawl with "Beans and weenies, taters to gobble up 'cause I got to pay for my fuckin ford." Carolyn pinched my arms for me to shut up. And I did. Not because of them but because Chacon was in trouble. Mancini had him in the corner, sticking hard and deep into his face. Stay up, little man, I said to myself. Don't go down. But Mancini pumped hard and Chacon pumped back slowly as he slid along the ropes. Then it was over. Tony Perez, the referee, stepped between them to stop the fight.

I forgot the heavy guys and they forgot me because Chacon, *our* Mexican, our California kid, our baby-faced boy wonder, was on one knee and not getting up. We watched the replay of the third round: the overhand right, then the stiff left, then the right again. A leg buckled. Blood sprayed like glass from his face and his smile of the early rounds turned to a wince. We watched the replay again, then a third time, before I chugged my beer and led Carolyn to the door, thanking the bartender as we walked past the long, almost empty, bar counter. In the night air I was still troubled. How could he lose? He was on our side, I told Carolyn as we crossed the street against a red light. He couldn't lose. He was one of us.

We hurried across the street to Captain Video and,

even though we didn't own a video recorder, scanned with other couples through the movie selections. It didn't make sense, our being there. But neither did Chacon's loss. He was our blood, a genius of the heart, and no way could he go down without getting up. We looked around for a while and then trotted back across the street for another drink to see if his loss made sense.

Expecting Friends

MY FRIENDS are coming—Jon the Estonian and Omar the Mexican—and what we want is to sit under the apricot tree in the backyard and talk about friends who couldn't come—Chris the one-book scholar and Leonard the two-beat drummer. We're going to talk poetry, ours mostly, and open beers one after another until we're a little drunk and a little wiser than the chairs we're sitting on. But we're going to take this slowly. We may, in fact, not sit under that tree but first take a drive to Tilden Park, where we'll hike as if there's a place to go and maybe sit waist-deep in wild grass, chewing long stalks that are springboards for the ants. Later we could go the Country Club and slouch in leather chairs that overlook the green and its small rise of hills. Men in plaid kneeling over golf balls. Clouds over the trees. Trees like pieces of the sea standing up. The day will be so open, so filled with blue air, that we won't believe it's all for us.

But who are these friends? Jon was a classmate in poetry, roommate in Laguna Beach, and the best man in my wedding, a guy who drank to all the causes of the heart. A friend writes of Jon and the day of the wedding:

The best man, lifting
at least his fifth bottle of champagne,
stands on a table in his white tuxedo;
and turning slowly toward us, like Tommy Dorsey
to the band, invites us to toast the moon,
the clear Fresno moon, which he finds gone.

And the moon did disappear, for my wife and I married on a night of an eclipse that comes every twenty
years, a rare treat for the astronomer's wife. We
didn't know. We planned the wedding from an old
calendar, sent out homemade invitations, and stood
in front of a churchroom of relatives who gave
money, clock radios, vases, a quilt, and a new bed to
wear down over the years. Here are sensible gifts,
they were saying. Now make a home. Make a laughing baby in your arms.

And Omar? He was already a poet when I was a
naive college student who carried books under both
arms when we first met in a hallway at Fresno State
in 1972. I put down my books and asked, "Are you
really Omar?" He smiled, offered a clammy hand,
and said, "Keep reading, young man," when I told
him how much I admired his poetry. And I did. I
read lines like, "Someone is chasing me up my
sleeve" and "If I remember the dying maybe I'll be all
right."

Later in the year I saw him with friends in front of
the student union. Omar looked tattered, like a sailor
roughed up by the sea, for his face was stubbled, his

eyes red and milky in the corners, and his hair stiff as a shirt collar. I joined him and his friends who were hunched in old trench coats, feet moving a little because it was a gray December. No one was talking or about to talk. They looked around like sparrows, heads turning nervously left and then right, and shivered the cold from their shoulders. I looked around too and shivered, shaking off the cold. Trying to be friendly, I asked Omar how he was doing. He turned to me with a crazed look and said, "Go ask the dead!" I was taken back, surprised by his tone and half-eclipsed eye. Then he relaxed and chuckled; his friends chuckled. I opened my mouth into a stiff smile, stood with them for a while longer, and finally said goodbye as I hurried away with my sophomore books under my arms.

Omar the Crazy Gypsy, Lord Byron in Mexican clothes, cheerleader of the acid set of the late 60s, is now a quiet poet in the rural town of Sanger where, on weekends with an uncle, he sells pants, shirts, cowboy hats, and whatever workers buy from the back of a station wagon or sweaty tents at swap meets. He is a merchant, he says, and when I ask jokingly if he sells his poetry too, he says, "Yes, they cost too. Right here." He touches his heart, and I know what he means.

These friends are coming to visit. We may drive to Tilden Park; we may drive across the San Rafael Bridge and search the water for migrating whales through binoculars. We'll pass the C&H Sugar Refin-

ery in Hercules, then San Quentin, and finally come
to the moss-green hills of Sonoma. We'll drive talking
and looking left, then right, between bites of apples
and slapped-together sandwiches. We may stop to
take pictures of cows; we may stop at a roadside bar
with a name like The South Forty or The Trail's End
and stand drinking frosty beers. After a beer or two
we may become so at ease that we invite a cowpoke
who, after two or three or four beers, may call us city
queers and hit us on our silly grins.

If we were smart we'd only drink one beer and get
out—or just stay home, my home in Berkeley, under
that apricot tree in the feathery light of an early
spring day. The world is in blossom: apple and apricot, the tulip and yellow daffodil that is broken by
wind. The sky is like no other: blue over the garage
and silver-blue where the sun is coming through behind a rack of clouds. The breeze is doing things in
the trees; my neighbor's dog is wagging his tail
against the fence.

This will be Saturday. I will get my winter wish: to
sit with friends who mean much to me and talk
about others who mean much to us. I've been waiting for this moment. I've been waiting months to
open up to others, laugh, and flick beer tops at kid-
ding friends who have drunk too much. We'll carry
chairs from the kitchen and set them under the tree.
My wife may join us; I'll slap my lap and she'll sit
with a sparkling wine glass in her hand. And our
daughter may come out with her flying dolphin, a

stuffed animal that's taped together and just hanging on. This will be Saturday, the weather faintly remembered from another time. In the backyard we may talk, or not talk, but be understood all the same.

LAST NIGHT I DREAMED about June Barrett, a girl from my high school. I dreamed that we were again side by side as we raced for A's in history. I felt her presence without looking at her. She was sitting with her back straight, hands quiet as flowers on her desk top, and legs pressed together as if she were holding a quarter between her knees. But she didn't need that coin. She could have opened up her legs and let it drop, rolling wildly until it flopped on its side, exhausted. Later, after class was dismissed, I could have picked up that quarter, bought a Coke, and dreamed about her with my eyes wide open.

She came from a good home in Sunnyside. A pool gleamed and rubbed light in her backyard, while a row of feathery trees bounced in the wind, casting shadows that made the grass seem even greener. Her mother was a mother in fine dress, not a fat terror with a folded belt. She stood over an electric range, stirring dishes I couldn't pronounce. "Filet mignon," she would say, "Consommé, capers, cornichons." When her family sat down to dinner, candles shone in their eyes. Their talk was soft. The music was soft. The food in their mouths was noiseless. They chewed, not chomped; they swallowed, not gulped;

and they asked for bread, not jumped with grabbing hands for the bigger pieces.

So it was June, the good daughter. June walking among autumn leaves with her best friend, June doing homework or talking with her father who could talk, not mumble with the TV on. June sleeping with a half-smile. June reading *Seventeen* while her childhood Teddy looked on from a high shelf, his eyes shiny as wet rocks.

Last night June Barrett came back in my sleep. She asked for me, said words, and almost touched my sleeve. She raised her hand when the teacher scanned the classroom. Answered Virginia 1808. Answered California 1949. Her hand shot up again, and again, and again. That was all. Some flashes in my sleep, light being thrown together to shape her face, the classroom, those years—and she was gone.

But I want to go back to high school and tell her things of my heart; how I walked through those days, thinking of her dresses, shoes, and lunches. I remember the happiness of her hair that bounced when she walked. She smiled the perfect teeth of magazines, the ones I scribbled black in my meanness, my bitterness, because her smile would get it all—the shiny cars, the houses, the beachfront vacations where she would sip tropical drinks with a lover or husband in the late haze of afternoon. The boy who cleaned up would be someone like me: brown, quiet, and so thin he would be hardly noticed among the chairs.

June, the bright girl, the college-bound mind among lesser minds—those who would become jani-

tors, warehousemen, and car salesmen in mis-
matched shirts, pants, and loud jackets. I was among
the lessers she never saw. I wanted to talk with her,
to sit near a splashy fountain and tell her about my
life or say something almost important. Look at this
about me, I would say. And look at this, and this.

The one time June noticed me was when my friend
Scott and I waited in front of the school for his
mother to pick us up. We leaned against the chainlink fence, doing nothing among the nobodies when,
to our surprise, then to our embarrassment, his
mother drove up in a truck the color of a pumpkin. A
banged truck. An Okie truck coughing blue smoke.
She called us above the engine noise. She jerked her
thumb over her shoulder, gesturing for us to hop in
the back. The cab was stuffed with tools, canvas
tarps, jacks, and tangled rope. What were we to do?
We were punk kids with tattoos penned on our wrists
and motor oil stinking up our hair. We jumped into
the back and at first felt foolish as the truck coughed
around the school, parading us for what we were
worth. I tried to crouch low but there was no place
to hide, unless I lay like the dead, face up and looking at the sky. But the bed was puddled with oil and
sticky as a shoe. So I squatted. I listened to Scott
laugh ignobly. I laughed with my hair full of wind,
laughed and thought, Who cares?

Maybe June Barrett cared. At the corner I saw her
in a station wagon, and she saw me before I had a
chance to turn my face away. She smiled like a
friend. I smiled back as the truck lurched forward so

that I had to grip the side or fall over like a bowling pin. That smile of hers stayed with me at the next intersection, and every other intersection for the next three years. I couldn't get it out of my mind—that smile that was more a reflex than a greeting.

From Scott's place I went home without hanging around to fool with his car, which was up on blocks in his backyard. I closed my bedroom door and listened to the radio for a song whose words I could steal and offer to June. But none came, fuzzy from the speaker. I got up, went to the backyard to kick a ball against the fence, and jumped that fence to walk the alley, first in silence and then quietly talking what troubled my heart.

June Barrett, June Flores, June Oda. They enter our lives like bright shadows and pass us up as they make their move for the good jobs and even better lives. They slip into business suits the color of money, and hurry-up steps, their hair bouncing from eagerness. They mother children. They host parties. They talk and make sense. Drinks are passed around from a serving tray, and their smiles, reflexes like springs, open up.

I dreamed about June Barrett last night. Her hands lay on her dress and her legs were pressed together. I saw this. And I saw her raise a hand for the teacher to call upon her. Even in dreams, she knew the answer.

Blue

HOW MUCH SKY do we need? If we're going to remain whole, healthy in mind, we need to walk, dream, lay inquisitively under the sky each day, or so writes a researcher who thinks neurosis arises from our disconnection from the sky. Look at the major cities— say New York or San Francisco—where the sky is often eclipsed by buildings, crossed up with wires, slivered and cut into pieces by bridges and towers, so that we can never look up to an unbroken sky. We get portions, flimsy postcards of blue, from where we sit at work or slouch at home. In such cities neurosis is prevalent, more visible daily than in places where the sky is not blocked out but fills the day and rains its complete, unfractured blue. Arizona. Montana. Canada. Those are the places. Australia. Africa. I only half-remember the places and don't recall how the researcher came to study this phenomenon, but I believed him.

When I was a kid of ten or so, a time when I could wander as I pleased, the sky seemed to show up more often, especially when my friend Jackie and I sat in fruit trees: orange, apricot, plum, and peach. We walked up alleys until we found one heavy with fruit half-guarded behind a wire fence and leaped so carelessly that sometimes we fell and got up with dust powdered on our eyelashes. We climbed trees and ate like birds, pecking holes in fruit that we dropped unfinished to the ground. We liked plums the best—the juice splashed against the insides of our cheeks and the roofs of our mouths. It excited us. When we smiled, our teeth were red and dripping.

After eating our fill we stayed in the trees to talk. And about what? Girls we were in love with, God, family, mean brothers on bicycles, school fights that did no one any good. As we spoke we seldom looked at one another. Instead, we looked skyward where, if it was spring, an occasional cloud chugged by, sloshing a belly full of rain, and if it was summer, the blue was the color of a crayon. I remember that well. I also remember Jackie and the beatings his father gave him, his body balled up under a bed and screaming *Daddy No!* I said these things too, and almost cried. Because we confided in one another with our eyes on the sky, we felt less troubled when we finally did drop to the ground and went back to our homes where, however slowly, it would begin again.

I remember the Fresno sky after a rain and how puddles flashed like knives when I walked past on my way to nowhere in particular, just looking about as I walked from my street into an alley, happy that I was outside and things were as clear as they were going to get in my young life. I walked toward Jackie's house, but instead of calling him I sneaked into his backyard, tore a couple of pomegranates from his tree, and raced down the alley to another friend's house.

When I called and no one came out, I climbed onto his pigeon coop and up onto the roof of his garage. There I tore open a pomegranate whose juice ran like fingers of blood down my sleeve to my elbows. While I ate I looked around until the sky seemed more beautiful than I remembered: the clouds were piled up, like fat Chinese faces and, from where I sat, the Sierras in the east were tipped white with snow and jagged like a child's scribbling. It was the first time I had seen them, snow or no snow, with so much blue behind them.

That was when I was ten. Now that I am so much older, the possibility of climbing a tree to eat fruit with a friend is almost nonexistent. How would I explain myself if someone, neighbor or wife, looked up among the ladders of leafy branches and saw a pant leg, a shirt, and finally a face, which would be mine. And what friends would climb for fruit they could enjoy on the ground?

But it's not a tree you need or a friend. It's the sky and the feeling that you're connected, that things are circular, beginning with the sky and all it holds: sun, moon, stars, wind, birds that come and go with the seasons.

I believe this more and more. Lying on a blanket at Tilden Park, I have listened to the wind in the trees recalling a childhood day, a friend, my wife, my daughter with clever tricks up her sleeve. I've lain half in shade, half in sun, and recalled all that I've enjoyed and, on occasion, have tried to clear my mind so that the sky is my only thought, its brightness like no other. When I close my eyes, the blue stays. When I listen to the wind, the blue stays. And a little green that makes me think of the sea.

Waiting

ONE DAY IN the summer that my father was to die, a bird flew into our house where it banged into walls and curtained windows. Its noisy beating scared my sister so that she ran to her bedroom until the bird was gone. We needed a broom, a dish towel, and Father's loud hisses to drive it away. It left by a window, perching outside on a wire, quickly shifting its black head in different directions. By the time I ran outside to throw a rock, it was on the neighbor's fence. The bird swooped away into a far tree, out of range. A month later, in August, father was dead from an accident at work.

This past July a bird found its way inside my sister's apartment. A window? An open door? We don't know. My sister had come home from shopping to find the bird on the dining table, its black stare like the one she saw years ago. Debra put down her groceries, careful not to disturb the bird, and opened the sliding glass door, the front door and windows. With a dish towel spread like a net, she slowly approached the bird that stared at her with an open beak. When she waved the towel, it flew and banged into the wall, letting loose feathers that slowly drifted downward. It flew again when she threw the dish towel and missed. Eventually the bird found its way to the porch where it stood profile so that one eye blinked at Debra. It blinked, jumped onto a rail, and was gone.

It was a death sign. Either someone was going to die, or the dead were present in the house, perhaps standing by the floor lamp or next to the chair where Debra sits to read the evening paper. The dead could press up to her face in sleep, and she wouldn't know. The creak from the bed could be the dead; the flash from the bathroom mirror could be the someone from the past. For the next few days she was careful. Work, people, and quiet intersections loomed in her mind as threats. She guarded her sons, not allowing them to go outside alone—or if they did, she watched from the window as they rode their bikes or played ball. She stood by, knowing that they might slip and fall and not get up.

And a week later, a robin flew into my house. I woke to a sound of things falling from shelves, and when I got up from bed a robin was at the front window looking out. It jumped, fluttered at the glass, and came down. It jumped again and flew into the bookshelves, dropping like a gray fruit to the floor.

I stood back, my heart racing, and I was so awake that my hair was lit with fear as the robin beat against the walls and windows. I opened the front door and went to the kitchen for a broom. When I came back I couldn't do anything. I sat on the couch watching the robin watch me as it strutted along the window, its claws clicking with each step. Finally I poked with the broom, so that the robin beat its wings and left by the window.

It was early morning—little after six—and a gray bank of clouds was pressed against the Berkeley hills. I went outside to try to follow the robin's flight, that crossed over the neighbor's house and out of view. I went back inside. Not knowing what to do, I returned to bed where I lay thinking of my wife and daughter and how the dead were in the house. I knew this. I closed my eyes and thought my father had come back to say something. He was here, or someone else was—a dead uncle in his tattered clothes. I listened to the house creak and the water heater fire up. When the morning newspaper popped against the porch, I flinched. I got up, dressed loosely in jeans and T-shirt, and went to the next room to see my daughter whose face was flushed pink from sleep. I went outside to the backyard to the study where my wife sleeps when she sews late at night. I rocked her hip to wake her, but stopped to hurry back inside when I thought that Mariko was alone. When I returned through the front door, the robin was standing in the fireplace looking at me. A chill ran like a zipper up my back. It flew awkwardly and banged the ceiling, and I hurried to get the broom.

The robin left by a window and didn't come back; for days afterwards I stayed home, venturing only to the backyard to watch Mariko play in a sand pile. I was careful in my movements. I picked fruit from the apricot tree only if I could reach them from the ground. I stayed away from work—hammers, shovels, ladders.

I listened to the house for signs. The creak of wood. Night breathings. The knock at the door and no one standing there when you opened. My sister came over the next evening. With my wife we sat at the kitchen table where we talked until we stopped to quiet our fear. I told her to be careful, not to do anything. These birds were either a death sign, the dead themselves, or maybe a curse (earlier in the summer, before Debra had moved to Berkeley from Fresno, she woke up one morning to find raw meat on her front steps. Pink meat on white butcher paper. A sign, our mother said, someone wants to hurt you).

Now these birds. Something is happening, I thought. I remembered that my father had died when I was five; my daughter was five that summer—my daughter who is so much like me in face and manner. And I'm like my father, in face and manner. I told my wife about these feelings, and she was scared, so troubled, that she couldn't sleep that night, and the next day she refused to let me go outside. I stayed in bed reading and listening for the house to tell me things. My daughter came often, with the *shish-shish* of her slippers, to read stories that ended in a happy life.

I waited all summer for that bird to come back and show itself as my father, gone so many years. I waited for him. I listened to the curtains move and the floor tick. Sometimes the sunlight on the floor—and even that cat who scratched a small hole in the yard and left it open—had meaning. I watched my daughter whose palm was mine, whose face was mine. I refused to let her go into the yard alone because he was there, just waiting.

"Don't come now," I said to Father all summer. Those days were so gray that he could have been anywhere.

White Blossoms

LAST DECEMBER I drove to downtown San Francisco to look for a gift for my wife, and no matter where I turned—left or right, up and down difficult hills—I couldn't find parking. The streets were clotted. Shoppers hugging awkward gifts in their arms jaywalked as they pleased without looking. Finally I nudged my car into a tight space six blocks from it all—I. Magnin, Macy's, Neiman-Marcus—and was walking with hands in my pockets and my jacket collar raised like a sail against the city wind when I saw three girls—third graders, I imagined—waiting at a crosswalk for the green light. Leather bags were strapped to their backs, and they were dressed in red plaid skirts, white blouses, and green sweaters—Catholic girls on the way from school?

Then I saw others, in twos and threes, and a stray one on a knee tying her shoe. I saw an uneven line of boys running after them and then still another group of girls. The boys caught up but stayed behind, almost in step but talking and laughing loudly.

These children brightened the gray day and the gray adult lives they walked among. I hurried after them because I was surprised to see them—school children in the middle of traffic, shoppers and tall buildings. I caught up with them but couldn't find the words to ask my simple question. I didn't want to scare them, to make them stop and ask why I was asking. They would have looked up at a stranger with windblown hair and dark skin, and would have turned away, hoping that I would leave.

I wanted to talk with them. I wanted to ask about their school and about themselves. Do you like the City? Where are your brothers and sisters? Which bus do you take home? A few days before I jogged on the track at Berkeley High and afterwards I sat, then lay with eyes closed, on the grass. Two girls about fifteen talked nearby, first giddy about a boy in their class, and then serious about their divorced parents whose lives were loose ends of old arguments. I listened and caught myself listening. This surprised me. I never thought I was so curious about others, especially teenagers with semi-punk hair. But I was. I caught most of their words and worried about their lives, even after the girls were gone.

I walked behind the children slowly, stopping now and then to peek into store windows—propped-up best sellers, winter clothes draped over chairs and ladders, kitchen knives hanging like threats by fishing line from the ceiling—so that I wouldn't overtake them. I walked quietly. I heard the girls spell "elephant," "rhinoceros," and "bureau." A spelling contest among themselves? A rehearsal for tomorrow's quiz? A girl in braids used her fingers to spell. With each letter, a finger sprung up like a fat, stiff worm, and went down again when it was needed for another letter.

I left them to their spelling and childhood laughter, and walked toward Macy's, still curious about them because they were so small, little kids in the rush of noise they call The City. The buildings, gray as a slate sea, dwarfed them and made them look fragile; the urgent taxis forced them to step back on the curbs and almost hold hands. The children were braving the elements and smiling through it all.

In the lingerie department at Macy's, I ran my hands over robes. I took one that I liked off the rack, twirled it on its hanger so that it flared open like a flower, and then checked the size, the price and the tab that said it was washable. I asked the saleslady about the color.

"White," she said, rubbing the cuff between her thumb and index finger. "This is just adorable!"

I stared squinting at the robe, and then looked at the saleslady. "No, no—I mean, is it a special white? Like 'egg-shell white' or 'apartment white'?"

The saleslady said it was regular white and, not wanting to risk another question, I bought it. And I bought a pair of slippers that the saleslady said, in an assuring voice, was also regular white.

With these gifts under my arm, I left Macy's and walked up O'Farrell Street in the direction of my car but in no hurry because I knew I still had time on the meter.

Again I saw Catholic students—not the earlier ones but others. They were walking in twos and threes, and almost huddled together like small-time conspirators. Again I had the urge to ask them where they were from, what school. I was amazed by their presence because it seemed so unlikely that a school would be pressed between the tall buildings of downtown San Francisco. I was more amazed that these children could maneuver among pushy crowds with such charge, with such confidence. The way they laughed openly and argued over this and that, it seemed natural to sidestep the poor man with his beaten cup and the streets burst open by jack hammers. They walked past the woman in a fur and the wag of a tight dress, and the men with money on their minds. They walked past it all, bright and talkative and natural as kids in the suburbs.

I wanted to talk to them, but I knew I couldn't because I wasn't their father, uncle, or older brother with a good job or generous wallet. I let them pass, my curiosity still itching like a palm, but thought of them as I walked back to the car, envying them because they went to school in a city I would have loved as a kid.

But where was the school? I walked and walked, and asked merchants in small shops if they knew the school. They shrugged their shoulders, sucked on cigars and let smoke issue from their lips. Some pointed gruffly toward Sutter. Others said they thought it was on Montgomery. I trudged up hills, around construction barriers, and even peeked into an alley, only to give up and return to a ticketed car. Sometimes you never find out. White blossoms fall at your feet, and you can only guess where they came from, what bright wind blew them your way. They sputter in the air, lingering against the blue, and then are gone.

Left Hand, Right Hand

I'VE STOLEN THINGS in my life, but it seems I owe so much more than I've taken. I first stole a toy car from the Japanese kid on our block who had everything. The second thing I stole was a box of maggots—or were they silkworms? To this day, I don't know what they were, except that they were white handfuls of movement in a box in the alley. I picked up that box and carried it home, hiding it in the bushes. I squatted and made small penguinlike steps into the cavernous leaves where I stirred the box with a stick as I tried to figure out what the movement was. Bugs? Baby chickens? Spider eggs? They were the size of fingernails, white and smelly. They moved as if they were trying to say something. This scared me. But I didn't leave or look away. I studied their motion until the smell overwhelmed me and I had to scramble out of the bush and into the house. I washed my hands and face, but the smell stayed. That night I closed my eyes, and the white movement stayed. The next day I returned to the bush and, with a quick peek inside, carried the box back to the alley. I hurried home to wash my hands and face, and listen to the radio to keep from thinking of what the white things were possibly saying.

After this adventure I was good for a month or so, but returned to taking things, like my mother's lipstick, which I placed in the street to see a truck smash it into a paste, and my brother's St. Christopher, which I tossed into our plum tree and forgot about, until only last week. Then I stole combs, earrings, and matches from the top of my parents' chest of drawers. I gave away my sister's shoes and let the dog have her sweater. I stole my cousin's Popsicle from the freezer but denied it, even though a yellow stain smeared my face like laughter. I was slowly becoming evil, but made a spiritual U-turn when I became a Catholic in the first grade. Once again I had become good and, consequently, guilty about my past. I repented, feared God. I made a resolution to stay away from my five-year-old sister, who went around on a sassy blue bicycle and cussed up a storm.

I was constantly tested. I saw fruit hanging from my neighbor's trees, red as sin. I fingered the loose change in the dish my mother kept in the cupboard. I held back playground punches and talked with girls about our Dick-and-Jane readers. Every Sunday I went to church, hands pressed together in prayer and head lowered. I looked at my shoes, occupied with the shine that I was sure everyone had noticed when I first walked in.

I remember one day when I was especially tested: it was a ritual for kids around our block to get together at a mom-and-pop store near our grammar school. There we bought penny candies: Tootsie Rolls, abba zabbas, jaw breakers, licorice that wagged from our mouths like donkey tails. That day I didn't have a penny. I went in but stood back watching the other kids argue and shout what candies they were going to buy. I watched them, enviously. Roy was rolling jaw breakers between his palms, waiting to pay. My brother was slapping a strip of black licorice against his wrist. I watched them until I could no longer stand it and squeezed between two other kids, placing my left hand on a Tootsie Roll and my right hand on a cinnamon sucker. Shame overwhelmed me, but I thought of the sweet bite that would roll in my mouth all the way to first grade. My hands started to close slowly over the candies, then opened suddenly. They started closing again, only to open more suddenly. My hands lay quiet on them, taking a rest. Then they closed again and this time stayed closed. But I couldn't move my hands away. They stayed on the candy rack, two quiet crabs, as my mind said Yes No Yes No. Finally it was a Yes and my hands pulled away from the rack. To my amazement the grocer, who had been watching me, said, "Two cents!" I looked up, scared. I didn't know what to do. I opened up my hands and there they were, two candies. I looked up to the grocer who was looking down at me, mean as a dog. I placed them on the counter. I told him that I also wanted to get a light bulb.

"What kind?" he asked, bluntly.

"A little one," I said, pressing my thumb and index

finger together and squinting at the air between them.

He showed me a shelf where the bulbs sat between sponges and dish soap. I said they were all too big and he pushed me to the counter where he showed me a tray of flashlight bulbs. I measured the bulbs between my fingers. Too small, too big, funny shape. None would do. I bunched my face with lines as best I could, and worried out loud because I needed that bulb real bad. He made a sour face. He slid the tray back under the glass case and told me to get the hell out of his store. And I did. I ran to school, with shame like a red stain of candy on my face.

Animals All Around

FOR MY CHILDHOOD FRIEND Jackie and me, there was no recognition of animal life, other than cats and dogs and an occasional squirrel that from a distance looked like a baseball mitt nailed to a tree. We lived on a broken block in a city that could come to an end only if you owned a car. You could drive to the foothills, and beyond to the Sierras, or to the crashing sea inspired by calendars given away by banks each December.

We had cars but went nowhere, for our stepfathers were beaten with work that made little money. On Saturdays they sat in front of the TV—robots of flesh with unblinking eyes—or mowed the lawn and set sprinklers that blossomed water in all directions. They gulped beers and thought of water: the sea with just enough wind, an umbrella, a spread blanket, and an ice chest of sandwiches and beers.

On Saturdays, knowing that we were not going anywhere, even though the television said we should go places—Beav and his family in white clothes on a picnic and Fred MacMurray tapping his pipe on a redwood tree at Bear Mountain—Jackie and I got together in an alley behind my house to climb trees and believe we were somewhere special, Yellowstone or the Grand Canyon.

What do you see, I would ask, and he'd push me and speak in a whisper: bear, deer, beaver thing. I looked where he pointed, gawking like a fool, and shot whatever it was dead. They were put to good use: flogged into hamburgers, skinned and shaped into furry coats that dwarfed our small faces even more.

Sometimes we went farther: Africa. Lions sunned on rocks and rhinos, muddy as shoes, stood knee-deep in grass. We shot them with our fingers shaped into pistols. But they only blinked. It took an arm, stiffened into a bazooka, to open their eyes and send them running.

But we didn't go to Africa often. We stayed in America with our own animals. We stayed in the trees, Saturday after Saturday until, finally bored with it all, we climbed down from the trees and begged and cried to go places where animals might be. Our fathers told us to get the hell out of the house and our mothers, subtler but just as tough, made their eyes big with anger and threatened to make us rake leaves or weed a flower bed—the hard labor of childhood. We ran out of the house, scared of work and the meanness behind their eyes that threatened to activate their spanking hands.

When this happened Jackie and I took off on our bikes to Roeding Park. We stood at a pond, frothy green with algae and dotted with milk cartons. With a stick we tapped the cartons to the edge, only to throw them back when two black kids, in T-shirts that ended at the belly buttons, warned us to leave them alone. We threw them back, scared but ready to run them over with our bikes if they gave us trouble. But they didn't. They asked if we were brothers. I told them I was Mexican and Jackie was Okie. We passed questions back and forth, and then rode off to the zoo, stopping first to climb the Sherman tank, a monument to WWI behind a chain fence spray painted gold, and then to scan the horizon of picnickers chugging sodas in the afternoon sun.

At the zoo, we locked our bikes to a parking meter and hurried to the entrance where we tried to walk in without being noticed. But we were pulled aside, almost roughly.

"It's a dime," a man in a blue coat said.

We walked away without the usual routine of patting our pant pockets or blaming each other for the lost dime. We hurried around the corner out of view of the gate keeper, thinking of what to do. We stopped in our tracks when we heard the elephant trumpet. Jackie looked at me, and I at him with an exaggerated excitement. We punched each other in the arms and raced around the zoo, looking for an excluded place that would allow us to climb the fence. We found one near the garbage bins. On our knees we pressed our faces to the chain links. We saw leaves and smelled a rudeness that puckered our faces. Still, we started climbing, our fingers gripping the fence hard as we scaled upward. At the top we rested and scanned the trees for monkeys that might drop on us. We saddled the barbed wire carefully, our crotches almost nicking the wire. I swung my leg over, frightened as I ever was and even more frightened when I spotted an ostrich strutting in our direction.

"Look," I said to Jackie. He looked where I was pointing. He crossed his eyes at the ostrich, then lost his footing, so that his body stuttered down the fence, with a rope of blood following. He got up, stunned by the fall, and crying because blood was bubbling from his wrist.

An animal keeper, with buckets in his hands, hurried over yelling why in the hell he was fooling with the ostrich. He peeled Jackie's hand from the wound, and blood flecked his shirt like a fountain pen gone haywire. He backed away with a "Goddamn kid." He pulled a handkerchief from his pocket and again peeled Jackie's hand away to tie the slash closed. He looked up at me. "And what you doing up there?" Fear caught in my throat. I almost started crying but wised up. "I saw this kid fall," I said, "I wanted to help—swear to God!"

But he wasn't listening. He turned to Jackie and pushed him in the direction of a gate that would lead to the emergency room and maybe the cops who could come to get me. I climbed down, raced to my bicycle, and rode back to the Sherman tank where, on top, I waited for Jackie to come out with a white bandage, big as a flag, tied to his arm. I waited an hour and when he didn't come out I rode home with a chicken bone of fear poking my throat. At home I tried to be good. I went outside and began pulling weeds from the flower bed. I raked the alley. I took out the garbage. At dinner I used my napkin fourteen times and ate slowly as I made conversation. Then it came: the phone call from Jackie's mother. I sat in the bathroom. I heard my mother say, "Oh these kids, if it's not one thing it's another."

Then she hung up. A moment of silence passed. I heard her sneak to her bedroom and search the closet: a thin belt doubled in her hands? She walked on tiptoes to the bathroom, then pushed hard, thinking that she would catch me off guard. No such luck. I stood behind a locked door, begging.

"Mommie, listen," I cried, "Jackie did it, not me. He wanted to see the elephants, and I told him not to do it." I could sense her eyes burning holes into the door. Fear crawled my back like a fidgety fly. She rattled the door, yelled, sweettalked me with a mouthful of Juicy Fruit gum. She slapped the door with the belt and pounded for me to open up. But I refused. I remained in the bathroom shivering and praying for a way out other than the door. Then I made my move. I pulled open the door and dashed for the living room, thinking all the while that some-one—brother or irate mother—would pounce on me. But no one stopped me, except myself. I peeked out the front window. Mother was on the front lawn talking with my Aunt Frances. I stepped onto the porch, quietly closing the screen door behind. When my aunt wriggled hello with her fingers, my mother, whose back was to me, turned to look over her shoulder.

"I'll take care of you later," she said and went on talking with my aunt. I carried my limp soul to the alley, climbed into a tree, and searched the places where Jackie and I saw animals, big animals that could take care of the world and save a kid's life against all mothers.

My Nephew

MY NEPHEW. My sister's boy. He's four and some months, hair full of wind and trouble. The other day I caught him pinching handfuls of pennies from the ashtray in my bedroom.

"What are you up to?" I asked.

"Getting rich," he said. He smiled up at me, looked down with a mixture of fear and comedy rubbed into his face, and wiped a few sweaty pennies from his palm back into the ashtray. He walked away, back to my daughter's room—my daughter who was in her reading corner, hiding I suspect, because she too had a few pennies pressed like dark stars to her palm.

His name is Diego, but he also goes by the name of Popeye. Some day he just may become a sailor, for already his body, with its small shadows of muscle, is squat as a suitcase. When he's shirtless and hangs from the trapeze in the backyard, the muscles in his arms show themselves like tiny, unripe apples as he does chin ups. He lets go, grins like he means business, and runs around in search of something to whack with his rolled-up newspaper sword. Then he comes back, breathing hard and bobbing like a

clown, and opens his palm for a penny in payment
for his little show.

But Diego can be quiet and even a pleasure. With
Mariko he will cut pictures from magazines and
paste them on construction paper. While they work
in the bedroom, the only sounds that issue from them
are busy scissors and simple requests: "Gimme the
paste." If somebody peeked into the room, he might
think they were dwarf monks restoring a medieval
manuscript—inking gold leaf on the corners of pages
brittle as dead insects. They are quiet, absorbed in
play and out of my hair.

Diego is the kid who pours sand in my daughter's
hair, looks around with his tiny grin as she starts up
her machinery of tears, and pours again. I know him
as the kid who falls and laughs but cries when his
mother leaves for work, his mouth open as wide as a
doughnut. I could saucer one into his mouth, and
that would quiet him, make him chomp down on the
sweetness of life.

He's a strong but small kid who one day may run
track, dance or twist his way to fame on the parallel
bars. I can see him doing any of those, or even boxing, for there's a clear vein of meanness in him that
may make him enough money to keep him away
from the pennies in my bedroom.

But that day is years away. For now, I'm trying to
teach him the ABCs. Last night we sat at the dining
table studying the first seven letters of the alphabet.
With Diego in my lap I sang and hummed these letters over and over, thinking if he heard their names

enough they would make sense. I sang, and then he sang. When I thought he was ready, I asked him to say the letters by himself, but he grew quiet as he had no idea of what to say. He scratched at the letter D, as if he wanted to get rid of it. I squeezed his hand gently and asked him what this letter was, pointing to the A.

"G," he said. I said, "No, an A."

A few seconds later I asked him again, and that time he said, "W." Again I corrected him and squeezed his hand away from half-hiding the alphabet. We moved to B, then C, then D, and with each letter he stabbed in the dark, guessing once that the D was the number four.

But we practiced, and some of it sank in, because by the end of our half-hour session he could say the first three letters of the alphabet. I was pleased with this start. I made myself a cup of coffee and bragged to my wife that I was going to make Diego into a little scholar. She smiled and ushered the kids into the bedroom to put on their pajamas. I went to the living room where I put my feet up on the couch and listened to them in the bathroom brushing their teeth. My wife joined me, her head like a tired moon on my shoulder. I listened to Diego gargle water and heard Mariko say, "Lookit. I got it for my birthday." I knew she was referring to a fancy soap pressed into the shape of a rabbit.

"What dat?" Diego asked. "An alarm clock?"

I laughed, splashed coffee on my robe, and knocked my wife's head gently with a knuckle as she rolled her eyes back. Diego ran by the door, happy as you can get in this life, and, fingers like a gun, shot *bing, bing, bing*. In bed we lay with arms behind our heads as we blinked at the ceiling, wondering about this kid who was in bed in the dark whispering, "Uncle, uncle, I got a nose."

On Our Own

MY DAUGHTER AND I are fending for ourselves. Yesterday we went to Golden Gate Park where we visited the Steinhardt Aquarium. We looked at lizards and toads that looked at us from their backdrop of sand and dead limbs that were supposed to be trees. But the toads, peppered with green spots, refused to meet our happiness no matter how often we tapped our fingers on the glass and laughed at the flies crawling on their squat heads.

I carried Mariko in my arms when we walked over to the pond and its false waterfall, half-hidden behind flags of broad banana leaves, which were real. Alligators were there, gluey-eyed and seemingly dead. The turtles among them were busy in the pond, though. They bicycled their feet, bobbed in the waves they made, and climbed steadily up difficult rocks. Mariko enjoyed this; I smiled and ushered her toward the dark hall of fish tanks, stopping at each one for a glance.

But we stayed to watch the penguins, new acquisitions, turn sweetly in our direction, as if to say, "Hello to you!" They waddled, they dove into the greenish water, they faced each other like friends at a cocktail party. Mariko turned to me, utterly charmed. I smiled some more, thinking how much I wanted to be home with a beer and the TV turned on to just about anything. But I checked my greed. I whispered in her ear that she was sweet like them, this four-year-old who later at home would waddle like a penguin and dive into the couch, making the sound of water splashing.

So it was. We looked at fish, or what looked like fish, and wandered in the nature room where deer and beavers and antelope stood glassy-eyed and stiff in their fur. After this we went outside. We ate lunch on a bench and watched sparrows, those hoods of the air, bicker over spilled popcorn. They bobbed, they jabbed at crumbs, they scratched at the ground and fluttered their gray wings for no reason at all. We ate our sandwiches and, when we had had enough, we saucered the uneaten bread. They pounced on it, making noises that made passersby turn to see what was happening.

From there we went to the racketball courts behind the museum. The Saturday crowd was there: Ronnie, Eliot, Hiro, Carlos. They were shirtless on the bench, sweat like a yellow mist on their faces, while someone, who was only a familiar name, was talking about a talent show he had seen in the Mission. He stopped, however, when he saw me coming. The crowd greeted me with a "Hey dude" and my daughter with a handshake.

Mariko stiffened and averted her eyes, looking down in shy posture. I picked her up, bounced her in my arms, and told these guys that she was my daughter. Unshaven and almost seedy, Carlos said, "Wait a minute," and searched his backpack for an orange. He pulled out beers, a bag of sunflower seeds, balled socks but no orange. He shrugged his shoulder and asked if I was ready to play. I said no. I told him that my wife was out of town, that I had to take care of my daughter. And anyway I hadn't brought my gear.

We talked for a while and then left them, these ragtag men who waved bye-bye until we were out of sight. At home we played in the sand pile in the backyard. By then Mariko's nose was running and her knit hat was stuck with leaves because she had fallen so many times.

We went inside. When I took off a shoe, sand hissed on the floor. I was careful with the next one, and careful when I tugged off her pants for there was no telling what was going to fall out. I slipped her into pajamas and a robe, and went into the kitchen to start dinner. I opened the refrigerator and a harsh light glared at me. I looked inside the meat drawer: a round steak, breakfast sausages, hamburger, cheese, and more cheese.

I fried the sausages, cut planks of swiss cheese, and fixed two pickles on each plate. I made toast to make sandwiches. I scooted Mariko into her high chair, and we ate noisily, happy that we were home in spite of Carolyn's absence because there was something about the hour, the dusk settling in the streets, our neighbor raking leaves while other leaves were still coming down. I made another sandwich to share but left that one cold because we remembered the ice cream.

But our jaunty mood changed. After dinner Mariko stumbled on a throw rug, jamming a finger when she went down. I soaked her hurt under cold water as tears leapt from her eyes. I rocked her in my arms, cooing love words that quieted her so that she almost fell asleep. But she came back to life when I asked her if she wanted ice cream. I carried her to my bedroom, turned on the television to "Wild, Wild America," and went to the kitchen to measure ice cream into tumblers, seeing that most of everything was in the sink.

We watched her program, or tried to watch it because her demands grew: more napkins, a glass of water, a bigger Band-Aid for her finger, her stuffed dolphin in its homemade sleeping bag. I did a puppet show with her dolphin as the lead, but she was unmoved by my story of the motherless family with a barbaric deportment.

This was us, of course. Carolyn was gone, and the house, usually clean and steamy with kitchen smells, was a shock of strewn clothes, unwashed dishes, and odd smells that banged you out of nowhere.

After I put Mariko to bed, I began to pick up, but forgot all about my task when I found an article in *National Geographic* about otters so fascinating that I took it to bed with me immediately. The next morning, or what appeared to be morning, for it was still dark outside, Mariko shuffled in her slippers to my bed. She climbed in, asking about breakfast, and I was too tired, too out-of-it, to say a sentence to appease her hunger. When I opened an eye, she was sucking her thumb and running a tiny hand in my hair. She then moved a careful finger to my crusty eyes and peeled a few crumbs from the corners. I rolled over, groaned, and tried to stretch life into my body. I got up quickly, thinking perhaps that might do the trick. But it only made me dizzy. I fell back. I wrapped the blankets around my head and asked Mariko, "What if Mommy never comes back?"

Worry did something with her forehead. She stopped sucking her thumb, swallowed, and said, "I don't want to think about it." I didn't either. Someone had to save us. I shut my eyes but opened them wide to greet the new day. Mariko peeled more crust from the corner of my eyes and said that I was a dirty daddy.

The Talking Heads

EACH OF US is less a person than when we started off on our knees, and each of us has torn out parts of the heart and sold them for good lives, or bad lives, but sold them all the same. We lose that child of the heart by becoming adults who compromise their dreams for jobs, for grades, for small pay raises that may buy pants or skirts, shoes or feathery hats that cover up the shame.

One summer when I was out of work, I said to myself that work was for fools, and since there were enough of them in the world I was going to become something else—a reader of serious literature. So what was there to do? Drink water with my friend Leonard Adame and play backyard philosophers, sophists of the lawn chair and the bruised tomatoes. We conferred greatness on Garcia Márquez and Günter Grass, and handed out trophies to Neruda, Herbert, and Pavese. We pinned ribbons on Sherwood Anderson, Knut Hamsun, J. F. Powers, and Carlos Drummond de Andrade. Come back player of the year: Nazim Hikmet. Inspirational leader: Miguel Hernández. Rookies of the year: Us! Adame and Soto, with 44 home runs each.

We talked politics, that foul fish for the cat, and

made sense. We talked movies, Europe, and movies in Europe, until we were so excited by our talk that one night we bought beer and sat in the yard at dusk, when the heat of Fresno began to settle into the 80s and the evening light was a filthy pink, then a gray. That night we talked about educated Chicanos, those graduating from universities but falling for the "new car" and the "tract home on the Northside." The adults were playing "Disneyland for the kids, Reno for us." It was a simple game, like Rummy or checkers, and those who were intelligent, somewhat ambitious but not aggressive, and not terribly bad to look at, could play it. For them, it was a thrill to flip open a check book at a fashionable clothing store and produce a driver's license and two credit cards. Though we talked and made some sense, we didn't say aloud that we were tired of this poor life and, if we had the chance, we too would grab the good jobs and go water skiing on the weekend.

Leonard adjusted his glasses and started with a flippant observation. "Soto, not even the dolphins are safe. Let one get out of the water and watch TV, and man he'd have himself a credit card in a minute. Beachballs for that guy."

We went on talking for an hour before I suggested that we have breakfast at the Eagle Cafe. I reported through the bedroom window to Carolyn who was sewing a new dress. "OK, you drunks, but be careful," she said without looking up or breaking her rhythm at the sewing machine. I stepped back from the window and looked at Leonard with a drunken grin. "Yes, we must be careful. The waffles at the Eagle are deadly." The cafe was three difficult blocks away. A few beers tumbled my mind and ten or so weighted Leonard down like an anchor.

The Eagle Cafe was a sad place, frequented by used-car salesmen, mental patients, and old merchants in plaid jackets—those trotting through bad times. The cafe was a "greasy spoon" where, in fact, it was possible to slip on the greasy floor and get hurt. You had to walk cautiously—or wear baseball cleats.

We had breakfast and talked baseball, then football, then baseball again until we returned to serious talk—politics. But soon this grew tiresome. We returned to talking sports and then on to love affairs that were so convoluted that they were like novels we couldn't put down. But eventually we did put them down, pay, and start back to my apartment, poor friends of the same mind. We walked without talking, exhausted from the late hour and too many beers. In that moment, we were so close in our thinking that we were almost the same person, but only walking in two bodies in different places.

When we arrived at my apartment, we sat on the front steps and opened yet another beer. Crickets made noises in the bushes and in our heads. The porchlight threw a yellow glow that did very little in that dark of broken-down apartments. We sat looking straight ahead. We thought about how our lives could end here in this back apartment and how nothing would change. A dog crossed the street in our direction and barely looked at us as he passed in his search of toppled garbage cans and a good time. Leonard smiled, shaking his head. "More people know that damn dog than us." He sucked at his beer until there was only air, then threw the empty bottle at the hedge where the crickets had once again started up their machinery.

"Shut up there," he shouted, and the crickets quieted. The ringing in our heads kept on all that night and into the morning when we woke to a new day that was dressed in the same clothes.

Pulling a Cart

I REMEMBER A MAN in overalls with a rope over his shoulder, weight slanting like a rickety fence, pulling a wooden cart onto our street. In the cart a woman sat queen-like, swaddled in bulky sweaters and two or three skirts the color of clay. Her face was also clay colored: bitten face of hard years, an unlit pipe cold in her hanging mouth. Husband and wife, they rattled our way in search of paper and glass, broken clocks and radios, heads of lettuce from garbage cans that we set on the curb on Wednesdays. Fruit beckoned them into our yards. Figs filled their hands and oranges bobbed on high limbs. They camped in alleys, lit small stick-crossed fires, and slept under trees. If it was winter and raining, they pulled a tarp over their heads, hunched together sitting up, and blinked like birds all through the night.

But they turned onto our street only in summer, it seemed. If we were inside, we kids looked on sadly from the front windows. If we were outside, we half-hid behind bushes or skinny trees to watch them pass. They didn't bother to look around. The husband faced the next street, indifferent to the neighbors peeking from behind curtains, and the wife, shadow-filled face down, played with a handkerchief.

After they passed we came out from hiding to watch
the cart rattle to the next block. They left and we
went on playing.

Husband and wife. That is what they were, living a
poverty that scared even the poor. And on our street,
a Mexican street with a few Okie faces, we knew
better than to taunt or point or feel ashamed of the
ragged. We were scared for them and, in a real way,
we were scared for ourselves because one day we
might have to pull a cart with a woman bundled in
so many clothes that we wouldn't know where the
cloth ended and the flesh began.

But as I grew older I became less shocked by their
presence in my life. I remember when I saw them on
the Fresno Mall. A girl and I were eating popcorn
and sharing a Coke when a noise started toward us. I
looked up. It was them: clay colored and bundled
deeper in rags. On that Saturday, I was in love and
trying to be a man of thirteen with two girlfriends
already behind me. When I saw the cart making its
way toward us, I made a sour face because they were
ruining everything. It was a spring day. I was in love.
I had money to buy popcorn and a Coke, and the girl
liked me enough to play with my sleeve. But still they
came, the cart rattling so loudly on its skates that I
momentarily lost that feeling of love, and forgot the
girl and the popcorn and the Coke that was by then a
rattle of ice in a cup. I looked away. I felt soiled to
see them. When they finally disappeared around a
corner, love wasn't the same. We pinched crumbs
from the popcorn bag. We scattered some for the

sparrows who bickered at our feet, like husbands and wives.

I won't be like them, I thought then, twenty years ago when I was a little man with a pretty date. Now I wonder. My wife is not centered on that cart; our daughter is not trailing us, vacant-eyed and hungry. No one is gawking; no one is pointing out our sadness when we take walks in the evening. But some days I feel as if I'm pulling a cart. My hands are frayed; the rope is frayed. The jars we collect along the way jingle like strange music and the newspapers, stacked and bundled, rustle in the wind of my pulling.

Some days my wife feels she's pulling me, in our tenth year of marriage, and no doubt our daughter, in her sixth year, feels that her pull keeps us together. We're making our way up this street, then that street. It's an effort that seems to take us no closer to what we want. The days end; dusk settles in the street. We never arrive.

Others are married, doing the same. They are pulling carts, weighed down with problems and finding no end in each step. It amazes me. I would think more would drop that rope and clop away in unlaced shoes, not looking back. But half of us stay, even if life is a pocketful of change, a cart, an apple and its bruised heart. We believe what we believe, and stay where we are.

Poor husband and poorer wife. I am amazed that we can be so human for only what we hold in our arms.

Taking Notice

MARIKO IS six and a half—or six and three quarters, as she often says—and is thirty-nine inches tall. Her hair is black; her eyes, slanted from a Japanese wind that's been blowing in my wife's family for 10,000 years, are brown and filled with light at almost any hour. She loves dresses and her stuffed animal, a dolphin the size of a hot dog, which she carries everywhere, even into sleep and watery dreams.

Her favorite holiday is Easter. There are things hiding in the grass—eggs and chocolates, a tiny gift to wear around her neck. Her favorite person is her mother. The second favorite person—herself. I'm number four, right behind our cat, Pip.

Mariko's a little philosopher in a starched jumper. After she jammed a finger against a chair and her mother told her that she should be more careful, she came back with, "How am I supposed to know the future!"

She's also blessed with tact. Once when we were stuck in traffic and her cousin was whining for this and that—Cokes, a restroom, more stick pretzels to smoke like cigarettes—she bent her five-year-old face to his four-year-old ear—and said in a whisper, "Diego, zip your lip."

Left handed. No scars. A little thin for a child who eats asparagus and artichokes, and everything else. The little space between her front teeth is marketable. When she smiles for the grandmothers, they fall over each other to open their purses and offer silver dollars for her bank.

Her greatest fear? Picking grapes. Her mother and I sometimes talk about that kind of work: the long hours, the wasps, the dust in the throat, the heat that won't go away. I say to her, "Mexicans are the people who pick grapes, and you're Mexican, Ronnie (her nickname)." She plays with her food, worry darkening her brow, and then she looks up hopeful: "I'm Japanese, too—they don't work that way, right, Mom?"

After school she reads, nibbles carrots for a snack, and follows her mother like a doctor from room to room. Since we have no other children, since there are no kids on our block, I often feel sorry for her, thinking she's missing out on something—friendship, fun, some fall from a tree that will help shape her character—and go out grudgingly to play a game with her, knowing that only nightfall or dinner will make her stop. On sunny days we stand in the backyard searching the flowery bushes for butterflies. I hold a homemade net; with two hands she grips a mayonnaise jar, with the lid off. We wait quietly for one to settle—poor creature that gets within range. I snap the net down, flick a yellow one into a mayonnaise jar, and later, at Mariko's insistence, pull off its wings to see what will happen. It always dies.

I'm taking notice. Today she's six and three-quarters, almost four-fifths, and already she's leaving us. She's putting on muscle and words and knowledge. Yesterday she came home with papers in her hands and said, "The vitamin C is in the skin of the grape, not the juice, Daddy." I didn't know that. And I didn't know how water runs uphill. She explained it to me with widened eyes and a flash of her tiny hands. I watched and listened, and would have given her everything in my heart, she was so sweet.

I'm a father and, like any father who's awake to his child, I can see her moving away. First it was her crawl, then steps, then words and whole sentences that have carried her this far. From a bloody cry on her mother's belly, she is now a little girl with colored pencils drawing her idea of what our house should look like. To her, we should have more trees —a ring of them making shadows everywhere. To her, we should add bedrooms where there is now an attic. We could see the bay from there. We're not far, she tells me. We're inching toward it each year—so say the scientists.

And summer this year? She swings like a lantern from the limbs of the apricot, and her arms color with the fruit. During the day, she's in love with the world from a plastic pool, and in the evening, her skin tingling from hours under the sun, she believes what she reads in bed. She's on her belly with her legs crossed in the air. I sit on the bed's edge to read to her. When she reads to me, I want to crawl into bed, tired from the day, and fall asleep to a story that always ends right.

She's almost seven. In another six years, she'll be as tall as her mother. Her skin will be a perpetual brown, the color of honey. Her body will be in bud: shoulders, breasts, the hip's curve like a mathematical equation that can't be solved. Her friends will be the same. They'll come over, quiet in my presence, in her mother's presence, but behind a closed bedroom door they'll laugh and gossip and share what there is to share in their 13th year.

I'm waiting for those years. I want to watch her play catch on the front lawn with a friend. They'll bend and stutter-step backwards. Their ponytails will ride the wind as they look skyward for a ball that will skip from their yapping mitts. I want to watch her sit among friends on the hood of my car. It will be summer when they talk about the nonsense of boys who won't go away. They'll giggle, roll their eyes, and cover their mouths to secrets that they'll half-remember a week later. They'll act big by themselves but small when they ask for money for an ice cream from a truck jingling up the street.

But I want the present, too, the little girl with scuffed knees and a stuffed dolphin. Let her tell me about vitamin C, dinosaurs, volcanoes, the Plains Indians. Let her ask me again and again for some sweet thing from the cupboard she can't reach. If there's nothing there, we can walk to the store. I take her hand for its tiny bell of warmth. At the corner, she asks, looking both ways and serious as she can get, "Now, Daddy?"

"Yes, Ronnie," I say, looking both ways myself. "Hold my hand tight. Don't let go." We'll hurry across, racing our shadows that seem so big that wherever we step is where we belong.

.

Saying Things

WE CAN SAY things but solve nothing. In a backyard I can say to a friend that the rain forests in Brazil are being cut down, raked clean of their goods, and bulldozed into smoke and a smoldering ash. The Indians there are giving up. Several years ago a tribe, appalled by it all, walked deeper into the jungle, banged their children and babies against the same trees where cities would go in the 21st century, and with machetes cut bloody shadows across their necks. The tribe vanished, simple as dust. They didn't want anything to do with us. Their desire was to die as a people, not as broken Indians pushed around for a small wage.

A tribe disappears in Brazil, another in Guatemala, still another in Thailand where the forests are standing open like doors for those who want to make money. The government bulldozes, shoves Indians into graves, and trucks lumber that will be hammered and glued into coffee tables bound for New Jersey.

There is more to this: if the Indians survive, if the forests survive, they'll be less than what they once were. Bunches of trees are stuck together and called a park, a national treasure by the Secretary of the Interior who has nothing to do with the existence of trees but is more than happy to stand by them when the picture taking begins. But in this forest roads snake through the trees, Coke bottles gleam in the grass, and graffiti of the worst kind—racial slurs, women with impossible breasts—is spray-painted on granite rocks, big as moving vans. Hot dog stands ring the forest, as if we need to eat before we sit under an umbrella of redwoods. Motels that look like log cabins stand at the gateway as if we need to sleep after looking at a bear buckle a trash can with his mighty paw. This is a park, we say to ourselves, to our children. We find it on maps—a shade of green, spread wide as a bruise—and we go.

Yesterday Pope Paul II gave mass to 40,000 Indians in Papua New Guinea. I noted a small number of these stone-age people, discovered only thirty years ago, was wearing T-shirts that said *I Love New York, Led Zeppelin,* or *I'm for Real*—or so I imagined on my TV. Most of the Indians were bright with flowers and pig grease, with necklaces of dog teeth, with feathers crowned on their spiky hair, raking the wind as they danced for His Holiness. But here and there, a T-shirt, an absurd pair of polyester pants on bodies that looked beautiful clothed with things picked from trees or shiny shells found on the ground. It's coming: in twenty years this tribe will run milky with disease and be flogged with debts for a patch of land that was once theirs just for living. Their children will ask, *What happened?* But it will be too late.

Nothing is solved. My friend and I can point to problems—cold sores in the mouth of the world. We can say this, and this, and this in his backyard, and not a goddamn life is going to change. We could, perhaps, get up and do something about the state of the world affairs. We can march shoulder to shoulder, with the anti-nuclear movement, with Greenpeace, with the Sierra Club, with the United Farm Workers of America's struggle to allow their people to eat more than platefuls of beans. In fact, we have done this. We have worked for such organizations and have done some good. Today we want an indirect life: we want to talk, to think about our fate, that blackness, that grave that will rain dirt on our faces and run a root through an ear until we can really hear.

This hand that speaks to a pencil, then a typewriter, can go on and on. I can say things that may solve a fingernail of pain—and isn't that a start? I can say what my friend and I talked about while we drank under a tree.

One, we should not eat more than two meals a day —the more there is for one person the less there is for another in a poor country.

Two, no income should be greater than another—a doctor should earn no more than, say, a janitor. Neither should earn enough to think he's permanent.

Three, all children should play until nightfall and read until they sleep.

Four, we should not wear more than is necessary.

Five, once a month we should walk until we become lost and must find a way back.

Six, curious minds should run the state.

This is what we talked about that night. Some of it is helpful. We would become better people if, for instance, once a month we drove to a place—city or countryside—and walked looking left, then right, as we took it all in. I've done this with a friend. We've walked through parts of Fresno we knew nothing about. We took in trees, rickety houses, new cars, people watering their lawns in the dusty twilight. I remember once on Pine Street we saw two kids, an Okie and a Mexican, taunting an old woman who was tottering up her porch steps. Maddened, we chased them until they gave up, cowering a little. We grabbed them by their filthy shirts, these poor kids with peach stains on their mouths, and yelled that we were going to bash their heads if we ever caught them doing that again to an old person. It scared them. They shivered like machinery before they said they were sorry and we let them go. They walked away, almost crying. We called them back and gave each a quarter to buy ice cream. They were crying by then, these kids that looked like us, only smaller. So this is what we were like, I thought to myself. Little boys. Cruel kids. We walked more miles to find others—and those old men with hoes in their hands.

We can say things but solve nothing. Today I've listened to a line in my head over and over: "the past seems horrible to me, the present gray and desolate, and the future utterly appalling." To me this bleak view is frightening. To another it's a sentence not to worry about. We believe our minds are singular and where we stand is the right place to be.

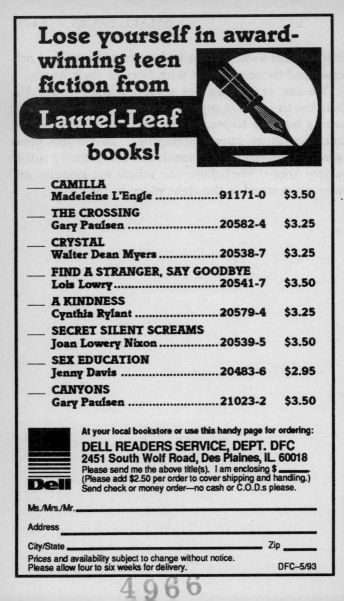
4966